Regulating Crypto

This book brings together experts from different fields and with different jurisdictional focuses to provide fresh ideas and deep insights into crypto regulation.

Cryptoassets engage many different areas of law, with their own specific terminologies, uncertainties and regulatory fragmentation. Unsurprisingly, then, crypto has faced calls for new laws, for reform of existing laws, and in some instances outright banning. Against this backdrop, this collection explores different aspects of crypto regulation, with reference to current developments, such as the Markets in Crypto-Assets Regulation, and technological innovations, including central bank digital currencies, smart contracts, and non-fungible tokens. Market, user and law-/policymaker perspectives are examined to explore not only innovation and opportunities, but also regulatory and policy challenges.

This volume will be a key resource for scholars and practitioners of law, finance, public policy, criminology and economics. It was originally published as a special issue of *Law and Financial Markets Review*.

Saskia Hufnagel is Professor at the University of Sydney Law School and Co-Director of the Sydney Institute of Criminology. She is also Senior Associate Research Fellow at the Institute of Advanced Legal Studies, University of London. Her research concerns global law enforcement cooperation, transnational and comparative criminal justice and art crime. She has worked at universities in both Europe and Australia. Saskia is a qualified German legal professional and accredited specialist in criminal law.

Colin King is Professor at the University of Sydney Law School, where he teaches and researches in evidence and financial crime, and is Senior Associate Research Fellow at the Institute of Advanced Legal Studies, University of London. Prior to arriving in Australia, he worked at universities in Leeds, Manchester, Sussex, and London (IALS). Colin is Editor-in-Chief of *Current Issues in Criminal Justice*.

Regulating Crypto

Edited by
Saskia Hufnagel and Colin King

Routledge
Taylor & Francis Group
LONDON AND NEW YORK

First published 2025
by Routledge
4 Park Square, Milton Park, Abingdon, Oxon OX14 4RN

and by Routledge
605 Third Avenue, New York, NY 10158

Routledge is an imprint of the Taylor & Francis Group, an informa business

British Library Cataloguing in Publication Data
A catalogue record for this book is available from the British Library

ISBN13: 978-1-032-94130-1 (hbk)
ISBN13: 978-1-032-94137-0 (pbk)
ISBN13: 978-1-003-56911-4 (ebk)

DOI: 10.4324/9781003569114

Typeset in Minion Pro
by Newgen Publishing UK

Publisher's Note
The publisher accepts responsibility for any inconsistencies that may have arisen during the conversion of this book from journal articles to book chapters, namely the inclusion of journal terminology.

Contents

Citation Information

The following chapters were originally published in *Law and Financial Markets Review*, volume 16, issue 3 (2022). When citing this material, please use the original page numbering for each article, as follows:

Introduction
Regulating crypto
Saskia Hufnagel and Colin King
Law and Financial Markets Review, volume 16, issue 3 (2022), pp. 177–180

Chapter 1
Digital payments system and market disruption
Andrea Miglionico
Law and Financial Markets Review, volume 16, issue 3 (2022), pp. 181–196

Chapter 2
Crypto payments – a danger to consumer protection?
Louise Damkjær Christensen
Law and Financial Markets Review, volume 16, issue 3 (2022), pp. 197–211

Chapter 3
Smart contracts: to regulate or not? Global perspectives
Pınar Çağlayan Aksoy
Law and Financial Markets Review, volume 16, issue 3 (2022), pp. 212–241

Chapter 4
Is the syndicated loans market ready for distributed ledger technology?
Hüseyin Can Aksoy
Law and Financial Markets Review, volume 16, issue 3 (2022), pp. 242–252

Chapter 5
The economic law of (central bank) digital currency
Filippo Zatti
Law and Financial Markets Review, volume 16, issue 3 (2022), pp. 253–265

Chapter 6

Regulating virtual asset service providers in the offshore world: the Cayman Islands example
Andrew James Perkins
Law and Financial Markets Review, volume 16, issue 3 (2022), pp. 266–283

Contributors

Hüseyin Can Aksoy, Faculty of Law, Bilkent University, Ankara, Türkiye.

Pınar Çağlayan Aksoy, Faculty of Law, Bilkent University, Ankara, Türkiye.

Louise Damkjær Christensen, Department of Law, University of Southern Denmark, Odense, Denmark.

Saskia Hufnagel, University of Sydney, Sydney, Australia.

Colin King, University of Sydney, Sydney, Australia.

Andrea Miglionico, School of Law, University of Reading, United Kingdom.

Andrew James Perkins, Truman Bodden Law School, George Town, Grand Cayman.

Filippo Zatti, Department of Economics and Management & BABEL, University of Florence, Florence, Italy.

Introduction: Regulating crypto

SaskiaHufnagel and ColinKing

There is rarely a dull moment in the world of cryptoassets, whether it is the price volatility of these assets; Bitcoin being adopted as legal tender (as happened in El Salvador); enforcement actions *by* regulators, as well as legal challenges *against* regulators' decisions (the US Securities & Exchange Commission being a prominent example); and regular criticism in political arenas (for example, linking crypto to terrorist financing). For lawyers, this field is both new and exciting with questions relating to the necessity of new laws, the reform of existing laws and the difficulties in the application of rules more generally. Also, many different areas of law are engaged in the regulation of cryptoassets – from contract law to securities law, criminal law to environmental law. In each of these areas of law, crypto raises numerous issues. In the criminal law context alone, there are concerns relating to, *inter alia*, money laundering; criminal hacking; fraud; and extortion.[1] A main issue in the legal context of cryptoassets is the lack of specific definitions. In the financial law context, there are uncertainties as to whether different cryptoassets constitute securities, while in contract law there are uncertainties as to the legal nature of new tools such as smart contracts. Furthermore, within the different areas of law, there is a danger of regulatory fragmentation where some jurisdictions introduce ad hoc legislation, whereas others adopt a wait-and-see approach. In recent years, there has consequently been increasing focus – from law enforcement, regulators, and policymakers – on the need for, and the form of, regulation in this sphere.

Not infrequently, there is reference to crypto being a 'Wild West'.[2] While in the EU, there is now the Markets in Crypto-Assets Regulation,[3] elsewhere there remains a lack of regulation and certainty (the US being perhaps an obvious example).[4] Even where there is regulation, not everything might be covered – for example, with the MiCA Regulation non-fungible tokens (NFTs) are, for now at least, excluded.[5] Uncertainties therefore abound: for example in the context of central bank digital currencies (CBDCs), do central banks have the authority to issue such a digital currency; can CBDCs be 'real' currency; and should digital currency be

---

[1] C Leuprecht, C Jenkins and R Hamilton, 'Virtual money laundering: policy implications of the proliferation in the illicit use of cryptocurrency' [2022] Journal of Financial Crime 12; C Cross, 'Romance baiting, cryptorom and "pig butchering": an evolutionary step in romance fraud' in *Current Issues in Criminal Justice*. DOI: 10.1080/10345329.2023.2248670.

[2] For example, House of Commons Treasury Committee, 'Crypto-assets' (HC 910) (September 2018), p. 33. See also F Panetta (member of the Executive Board of the European Central Bank), 'For a few cryptos more: the Wild West of crypto finance', Speech at Columbia University, New York (25 April 2022). Available at: https://www.ecb.europa.eu/press/key/date/2022/html/ecb.sp220425~6436006db0.en.html

[3] Regulation (EU) 2023/1114 of the European Parliament and of the Council of 31 May 2023 on markets in crypto-assets.

[4] See, for example, *Securities and Exchange Commission v Ripple Labs Inc* (SDNY, 22 Dec. 2020) Judgment: 13 July 2023 considering, *inter alia*, whether XRP constitutes a security or not. Also, in January 2024, the SEC approved a number of bitcoin exchange-traded funds (ETFs), though only after legal challenge: see G Gensler, 'Statement on the Approval of Spot Bitcoin Exchange-Traded Products' (SEC Statement, 10 January 2024). In *Grayscale Investments LLC v SEC*, No.22-1142 (D.C. Cir. 2023), 2 the Court of Appeals for the District of Columbia had described the SEC's initial rejection of the Grayscale ETF application as 'arbitrary and capricious because the Commission failed to explain its different treatment of similar products.'

[5] For wider consideration, see P Çağlayan Aksoy, 'The Regulation of NFTs: Much Ado About Nothing?' (2023) 44(4) Business Law Review 128. In the criminal law context, see S Hufnagel and C King, 'Non-Fungible Tokens: Art and Crime in a Virtual World' (2023) 5 Criminal Law Review 338.

legal tender?[6] As for smart contracts, how will this new development impact the traditional financial system; how might tensions be resolved?[7] Do digital assets constitute 'property'?[8] Thus, the law is constantly playing catch-up, not only in the crypto context but also with other technological innovations.[9]

Moving away from regulatory fragmentation, it is also important to consider the purpose of crypto regulation. The IMF Managing Director has said:

> Our goal is to make a more efficient, interoperable, and accessible financial system by providing rules to avoid the risks of crypto, and infrastructure by leveraging some of its technologies.[10]

In the UK, there has been significant attention on cryptoassets in recent years, including *inter alia* a Cryptoassets Taskforce,[11] Law Commission insights[12] and various parliamentary reviews.[13] In October 2023, it was confirmed that the government intended to move ahead with plans to regulate – to provide a regulatory environment that enables innovation but also ensuring financial stability.[14]

The chair of the UK Financial Conduct Authority (FCA) and Payment Systems Regulator (PSR) has suggested that legislators need to consider three issues when considering the role of crypto-regulation:

1. How to make it harder for digital tokens to be used for financial crime,
2. How to support useful innovation, and
3. The extent to which consumers should be free to buy unregulated (speculative) tokens and to assume personal responsibility.[15]

A HM Treasury consultation on cryptoassets highlighted the benefits of this technology, but continued on to say that 'these benefits can only be realised sustainably if the technology is adopted safely and accompanied by an effective and appropriate regulatory framework for

---

[6]These questions are explored in W Bossu et al, 'Legal Aspects of Central Bank Digital Currency: Central Bank and Monetary Law Considerations' (IMF Working Paper 2020).

[7]A Savelyev, 'Contract law 2.0: 'Smart' contracts as the beginning of the end of classic contract law' (2017) 26(2) *Information and Communications Technology Law* 116. Cf. M Durovic and C Willett, 'A Legal Framework for Using Smart Contracts in Consumer Contracts: Machines as Servants, Not Masters' (2023) 86(6) Modern Law Review 1390.

[8]Law Commission, 'Digital assets: Final report' (June 2023) 2: "most areas of residual legal uncertainty are highly nuanced and complex. That complexity remains, in part, because both the digital asset market and the technology in question is evolving and will continue to do so."

[9]For wider discussion on legal responses to technological change, see L Bennett Moses, 'Agents of Change' (2011) 20(4) Griffith Law Review 763. For consideration of the advantages and risks of early regulation, in the context of artificial intelligence (AI), see JM Bello y Villarino and R Vijeyarasa, 'International Human Rights, Artificial Intelligence, and the Challenge for the Pondering State: Time to Regulate?' (2022) 40(1) Nordic Journal of Human Rights 194.

[10]K Georgieva (IMF Managing Director), 'Leaving the Wild West: Taming Crypto and Unleashing Blockchain', Speech delivered at the MOEF-BOK-FSC-IMF International Conference on Digital Money, Seoul, South Korea (13 December 2023). Available at: https://www.imf.org/en/News/Articles/2023/12/13/sp121423-leaving-the-wild-west[1]kordigitalmoney. Emphasis in original.

[11]HM Treasury, Financial Conduct Authority and Bank of England, 'Cryptoassets Taskforce: final report' (October 2018).

[12]Law Commission (n 8); Law Commission, 'Smart legal contracts: Advice to Government' (November 2021).

[13]Recent examples include: House of Commons Treasury Committee, 'Regulating Crypto' (HC 615) (May 2023); House of Commons Culture, Media and Sport Committee, 'NFTs and the Blockchain: the risks to sport and culture' (HC 598) (October 2023). An All Party Parliamentary Group on 'Crypto and Digital Assets' was established in December 2021. See also s.69 of the Financial Services and Markets Act 2023 which provides a definition of 'cryptoasset'.

[14]H Jones, 'Britain to push ahead with rules for cryptoassets' (*Reuters*, 30 October 2023).

[15]C Randell (Chair of the FCA and PSR), 'The risks of token regulation', Speech delivered at the Cambridge International Symposium on Economic Crime (6 September 2021). Available at: https://www.fca.org.uk/news/speeches/risks-token-regulation

financial services.'[16] This stance was echoed by a Treasury Committee on regulating crypto: 'An effective regulatory framework would support development of such [*i.e. cryptoasset*] technologies in the UK, while also mitigating some of the risks cryptoassets pose.'[17]

Questions about regulation and crypto will not be alien to readers of this journal. Earlier issues have considered matters such as regulation in individual countries,[18] difficulties in applying existing payment laws to crypto exchanges,[19] anti-money laundering and cryptoassets,[20] and blockchain and trade finance.[21] This special issue brings together six original articles[22] developed from a two-day symposium held in London in October 2022.[23] Authors examine innovation and opportunities within the different aspects of the crypto-realm but also engage with policy and regulatory challenges.

The opening article of this issue, by Andrea Miglionico, illustrates the juxtaposition of such innovation and opportunities against demands for regulation. He demonstrates how new frontiers of money (including virtual currencies and crypto-assets) can assist with automated decision-making (such as anti-money laundering obligations), assist the underbanked, and promote financial inclusion. While such developments could potentially 'transform regulatory oversight', Miglionico expresses caution given the potential for prejudice, impacts on privacy, and concerns as to data security.

The second article examines the role of cryptocurrencies as a means of payment and the problems that arise for consumers when paying in crypto. By considering such problems against the backdrop of the MiCA Regulation, Louise Damkjaer Christensen explores possible regulatory solutions for the protection of consumers. She argues that the MiCA Regulation represents 'a missed opportunity' and that we are left with 'a legal vacuum of uncertainty for consumers', thus further regulatory action is needed.

Regulation in the crypto context is again a central focus in the third article, where Pinar Çağlayan Aksoy examines the regulation of smart contracts. Inevitably, this 'new' form of contract will challenge conventional approaches to, *inter alia*, formation, performance, jurisdiction and more, thus Aksoy asks whether smart contracts are *sui generis* as to require tailored regulation. Similar to the first two articles, she considers the balance between innovation and regulation (or protection of stakeholders). Regulation in this context is challenged by emerging technologies, including artificial intelligence (AI), big data, and distributed ledger technology (DLT) which, as Aksoy emphasises, are 'a challenge to existing legal taxonomies'.

Of course, smart contracts and distributed ledger technology have significant potential to overcome deficiencies in traditional financial markets. In the next article, Hüseyin Can Aksoy explores this potential in relation to syndicated loans. Indeed, he goes so far as to state that there is potential here to 'revolutionise' the syndicated loans market, particularly if used together. That notwithstanding, Aksoy acknowledges that there are difficulties and that

[16]HM Treasury, 'Future financial services regulatory regime for cryptoassets: Consultation and call for evidence' (February 2023) 7.

[17]House of Commons Treasury Committee (n 13) 18.

[18]CP Buttigieg and G Sapiano, 'A critical examination of the VFA framework – the VFA agent and beyond' (2020) 14(1) Law and Financial Markets Review 48.

[19]H Nabilou, 'The dark side of licensing cryptocurrency exchanges as payment institutions' (2020) 14(1) Law and Financial Markets Review 39.

[20]CP Buttigieg et al., 'Anti-money laundering regulation of crypto assets in Europe's smallest member state' (2019) 13(4) Law and Financial Markets Review 211.

[21]A Dahdal, J Truby and H Botosh, 'Trade finance in Qatar: blockchain and economic diversification' (2020) 14(4) Law and Financial Markets Review 223.

[22]There were to be seven articles but one article was mistakenly published in an earlier issue. See D Broby, 'Central bank digital currencies: policy implications' (2022) 16 Law and Financial Markets Review 100.

[23]This symposium was co-hosted by the QMUL Criminal Justice Centre and the IALS Centre for Financial Law, Regulation & Compliance (FinReg), funded by the Society of Legal Scholars (SLS) and the University of London Coffin Trust Fund.

there is a need for 'proper regulation' to ensure a predictable and legally safe environment in the context of syndicated loans and smart contracts and DLT.

Challenging the traditional financial system is also the focus of the fifth article, by Filippo Zatti, looking specifically at the digital transformation of money including cryptocurrencies, stablecoins, and central bank digital currencies (CBDCs). He highlights the differences between lawyers and economists in relation to 'money', and that these are exacerbated in the digital context. Traditional concepts such as legal tender; the nature of the economic and legal system; and sovereignty require new analyses in the modern context, or in the words of Zatti: there is a need for 'a re-evaluation of the effects of these changes on the concept of money as a public good and legal tender'. For example, he suggests that legal scholars have overlooked the impact of digital transformation, which has led to confusion amongst economic scholars.

The final article in this special issue is on virtual asset service providers, with a specific focus on the Cayman Islands. Cayman is, of course, a global financial hub, but the government also aspires to be a global technology hub. While wanting to be attractive to crypto companies, the importance of a sound regulatory framework is evident not least – as Andrew Perkins examines – given ongoing concerns as to the use of crypto in money laundering and terrorist financing. Perkins argues that the Cayman government 'has been proactive in seeking to attract [crypto] investment, but also to regulate it'. He specifically examines the Cayman Virtual Asset Service Providers Act to support his argument that Cayman is committed to compliance with international best practices. That notwithstanding, he expresses caution as to how the international community will view Cayman's efforts towards virtual assets not least given the complex regulatory questions that arise in this sphere. Moreover, he questions whether offshore jurisdictions are being held to higher standards due to their offshore status.

ORCID

Saskia Hufnagel http://orcid.org/0000-0002-3812-3183
Colin King http://orcid.org/0000-0001-8537-5853

OPEN ACCESS

Digital payments system and market disruption

Andrea Miglionico

ABSTRACT

The traditional banking functions of lending, deposit-taking and payment intermediation are being unbundled in the new frontiers of money that extend from virtual currencies to crypto-assets and from shadow payments to quasi-money. The possibility for digital-centred change in the financial industry is illustrated by distributed ledger technology, of which 'blockchain' is the most prominent example of automated decision-making. Other forms of decentralised supply of money, payment services, and funding processes may allow households and businesses to obtain loans and pool risks without having recourse to financial intermediaries. This article examines the alternative provision of access to low-cost zero-friction payments from the perspective of the underbanked. Promoting innovation through alternatives to credit means integrating vulnerable and excluded customers into mainstream financial systems. Blockchain technology backed by a possible modification of the law on the recognition and transfer of property rights might prove instrumental in unlocking the value of the assets possessed by the underbanked or even the unbanked.

A. Introduction

The digitalisation of payments systems has resulted in a large use of artificial intelligence (AI) applications, e.g. machine learning, neural networks and adaptive algorithms which automate decision-making processes while expediting the delivery of financial services.[1] Technology innovation assists firms' operating systems by supporting both risk assessment and peer comparison. But this can lead to problems. For example, where machine learning embeds manual intervention and the software for the algorithms on which the rules rely is not perfectly designed.[2] The Financial Conduct Authority (FCA) launched sandbox programmes to enhance oversight of prudential and conducts risks of fintech firms and incentivise collaborative dialogue between regulators and regulated firms.[3] This regulatory initiative has been followed by the EU Digital Finance Package,

[1]Nils J Nilsson, *Principles of Artificial Intelligence* (Morgan Kaufmann Publishers 1980) 2–3.

[2]Joseph Lee, 'Access to Finance for Artificial Intelligence Regulation in the Financial Services Industry' (2020) 21(4) European Business Organization Law Review 731, 738.

which includes an innovative programme, the distributed ledger technology (DLT) Pilot Regime for blockchain services.[4] The EU sandbox aims to establish a harmonised framework in the decision-making process between the DLT market infrastructures, the national competent authorities and European financial regulators.[5] The FCA also launched a regulatory 'scale up box', a second generation of digital sandboxes, to improve transparency in developing fintech products and systems of internal control.[6]

Access to digital technology supports financial inclusion and data sharing, which means banks provide financial services at affordable costs to disadvantaged customers. Whether technology-based forms of payments create the conditions to improve participation in the credit market among minority groups (i.e. individuals with disabilities and mental health issues, ethnic minorities, low-income households) depends on the design of firms' internal data and their operational and management information process.[7] This article examines the alternative provision of access of low-cost zero friction payments from the perspective of the underbanked. Blockchain technology backed by a possible modification of the law on the recognition and transfer of property rights might prove instrumental in unlocking the value of the assets possessed by the unbanked.[8]

The article proceeds as follows. The next section examines the digitalisation of bank business activities along with the digital transformation of payment platforms, and analyses which elements of regulation are potentially most easily automated. It explores whether automation of know-your-customer (KYC) rules and anti-money-laundering (AML) decisions (e.g. automated blocking of unusually large payments) are 'algorithm ready' and presented in a way which would allow automated software-based compliance. This raises the question of interpretation of data to ensure consistency and consensus in the automation process.

Section C considers regulatory technology (regtech) applications in the decision-making process of bank intermediaries and illustrates how they adapt to AI systems for producing information about modelling prudential risk and capital at risk for investors and regulators. Automated systems can incentivise a greater use of principles and judgement in regulation and supervision, even though the need to make the rulebook machine-readable might initially favour a shift away from principles, and towards rigidly applied rules. It also discusses the role of automated supervisory actions and how it will be affected by the use of algorithms to mitigate undesired regulatory outcomes, and whether artificial applications will reduce the role of human judgement in monitoring compliance with principles. Achieving the full benefits of technology in regulatory oversight will therefore require standardised access to institutions' operating systems and the data they contain. The opportunities provided by technology-based products can be used to transform regulatory oversight in ways that will yield far wider benefits than are sometimes envisaged.

---

[3]FCA, 'Regulatory sandbox' (2 January 2020), https://www.fca.org.uk/firms/regulatory-sandbox; 'The Digital Sandbox Pilot' (23 November 2020), https://www.fca.org.uk/firms/innovation/digital-sandbox.

[4]European Commission, 'Digital Finance Strategy for the EU' COM(2020) 591 final.

[5]Wolf-Georg Ringe and Christopher Ruof, 'Regulating Fintech in the EU: The Case for a Guided Sandbox' (2020) 11(3) European Journal of Risk Regulation 604, 622–23.

[6]Nikhil Rathi, 'Levelling the playing field – innovation in the service of consumers and the market' (20 April 2021), https://www.fca.org.uk/news/speeches/levelling-playing-field-innovation-service-consumers-and-market.

[7]Thomas Philippon, 'On Fintech and Financial Inclusion', NBER Working Paper 26330, http://www.nber.org/papers/w26330.

[8]Emily Lee, 'Financial Inclusion: A Challenge to the New Paradigm of Financial Technology, Regulatory Technology and Anti-Money Laundering Law' (2017) 6 Journal of Business Law 473, 498.

Section D addresses the main issues around the use of digital payments systems for vulnerable consumers and questions about potential discriminatory outcomes of algorithmic machines which can hinder financial inclusion. Using technology to improve the information available to investors and customers allows them to better observe and anticipate business decisions, and therefore ensures that these are desired outcomes, consistent with regulatory principles. The last section sets out some concluding remarks.

B. Digital financial intermediaries

The use of technology in the banking sector generally refers to algorithms in business decision-making both in investment contracts and in the business strategy.[9] Notably, the application of algorithms by financial institutions is used for automated risk assessment. Most algorithms operate within set variables, but self-learning algorithms operate beyond the control of their programmers, which makes the role of traditional mutual forms of traditional financial intermediary (e.g. building societies and credit unions) increasingly virtual rather than face-to-face.[10] Machine learning introduces automated agents such as robo-advisors and chatbots, although it is debatable whether they could ever have the same rights as a natural person.[11]

Regulatory technologies can increase the speed of client on-boarding and reduce risk as a distributed shared ledger acts as an immutable assured audit trail of all KYC processes and the automation of account opening.[12] Digitalisation of lending transactions through automated reading of data can enhance traceability of customers (e.g. verification of a customer's identity) and disclosure of information (e.g. KYC due diligence).[13] This could be particularly useful in the area of anti-money laundering (AML) and could mitigate the cyber risk of crypto assets being used for criminal purposes.[14] AML rules are inherently affected by technological platforms (e.g. data-mining techniques) which shape the regulatory framework into a data-based regime.[15] The EU Fifth Money Laundering Directive (5AMLD) provides for centralised automated mechanisms for bank and payment accounts to protect and verify personal data when carrying out AML investigations.[16] Specifically, the 5AMLD regulates central registries and central electronic data retrieval systems so as to allow timely identification of any natural and legal persons involved in suspicious

[9]Karen Yeung, 'Why Worry about Decision-Making by Machine?' in Karen Yeung and Martin Lodge (eds), *Algorithmic Regulation* (OUP 2019) 24–25.

[10]Andreas Kokkinis and Christian Twigg-Flesner, 'The potential impact of digitisation upon the regulation of financial markets and products' in Daniel Cash and Robert Goddard (eds), *Regulation and the Global Financial Crisis. Impact, Regulatory Responses, and Beyond* (Routledge 2020) 133.

[11]Roger Brownsword, 'Regulating AI and Robotics: The Questions that We Ask and the Questions that We Do Not Ask', keynote speech at the RIMA Workshop, University of York, School of Law, 15 December 2020. See also Belinda Bennett and Angela Daly, 'Recognising rights for robots: Can we? Will we? Should we? (2020) 12 Law, Innovation and Technology 60, 70–71.

[12]Yvonne Lootsma, 'Blockchain as the Newest Regtech Application— the Opportunity to Reduce the Burden of KYC for Financial Institutions' (2017) 36 Banking & Financial Services Policy Report 8, 16–17.

[13]Douglas W Arner and others, 'The Identity Challenge in Finance: From Analogue Identity to Digitized Identification to Digital KYC Utilities' (2019) 20(1) European Business Organization Law Review 55, 57.

[14]Iñaki Aldasoro and others, 'The drivers of cyber risk' (May 2020) BIS Working Papers No 865, https://www.bis.org/publ/work865.pdf.

[15]Dionysios S Demetis, *Technology and Anti-money Laundering: A Systems Theory and Risk-based Approach* (Edward Elgar 2010) 133–34.

[16]Recitals 21–22 in the preamble to Directive (EU) 2018/843 of the European Parliament and of the Council of 30 May 2018 amending Directive (EU) 2015/849 on the prevention of the use of the financial system for the purposes of money laundering or terrorist financing and amending Directives 2009/138/EC and 2013/36/EU.

activities.[17] The digital environment of financial transactions is exposed to cybercrimes, which makes the risk-based approach of AML obsolete and calls in question the need to develop automated regulation.[18] In this context, the use of technological applications can reduce the costs of intermediation by automating the collection, verification and transmission of required information to the regulatory authorities.[19] At the same time, it supports regulatory objectives by improving the accuracy and comparability of information, which would also enhance the ability of supervisors to monitor regulatory compliance.

Technology replaces traditional forms of financial intermediation by digital intermediary channels which aim to include underbanked and vulnerable customers in mainstream credit systems.[20] Access to financial services through sophisticated software has led to the automation of consumer platforms, notably crowdfunding (donation-based, reward-based and equity)[21] and peer-to-peer lending (P2P).[22] As a result, digital payments have reduced the role of intermediaries in evaluating the customer's profile and the suitability of products. Payment systems are closely linked to the broader impact of technology on the financial industry and public services and to wider issues of identity and data infrastructure (Paypal, M-Pesa, AliPay, WeChat Pay).[23] While there is a very large diffusion of data through digital investment schemes (e.g. biometric identification), there is relatively scarce understanding of the policy and practice applied to cyber security.

The growth of the P2P market, mainly driven by crowdfunding platforms, has provided investors with automated access to loan portfolios and created alternative forms of funds for consumers, although policy and regulatory issues arise with respect to potential systemic risk in this new business model.[24] In P2P lending mechanisms, users lend capital to borrowers and investors receive a credit claim to document the principal's commitment without recourse to bank intermediaries.[25] Lenders and borrowers interact across automated investment tools such as artificial machines (LendingRobot) which support the lender's search cost and allow private investors to compete with institutional investors.[26] Automated customer decision-making allocates lenders' funds automatically and assists

[17]See Article 32a of the Fifth Money Laundering Directive 2018/843.

[18]Douglas W Arner, and others, 'FinTech and RegTech. Enabling Innovation While Preserving Financial Stability' (2017) 18 Georgetown Journal of International Affairs 47, 52–53. The problem of cyber-laundering is discussed in Tatiana Tropina, 'Fighting money laundering in the age of online banking, virtual currencies and internet gambling' (2014) 15 ERA Forum 69, 82.

[19]Saul Levmore and Frank Fagan, 'The Impact of Artificial Intelligence on Rules, Standards, and Judicial Discretion' (2019) 93 Southern California Law Review 1, 12.

[20]Holly Powley and Keith Stanton, 'Financial conduct in the UK's banking sector. Regulating to protect vulnerable consumers' in Cătălin-Gabriel Stănescu and Asress Adimi Gikay (eds), *Discrimination, Vulnerable Consumers and Financial Inclusion. Fair Access to Financial Services and the Law* (Routledge 2021) 210–11.

[21]Donation-based, reward-based and equity-based crowdfunding are methods of financing characterised by the motivation of investment of funders and what they expect in return for their money. See Ivo Jenik, Timothy Lyman, and Alessandro Nava, 'Crowdfunding and Financial Inclusion' (March 2017), World Bank CGAP Working Paper, 5, https://www.cgap.org/research/publication/crowdfunding-and-financial-inclusion.

[22]Gareth W. Peters and Efstathios Panayi, 'Understanding Modern Banking Ledgers Through Blockchain Technologies: Future of Transaction Processing and Smart Contracts on the Internet of Money' in Paolo Tasca and others (eds), *Banking Beyond Banks and Money* (Springer International 2016) 239–40.

[23]John Engen, 'Lesson from a Mobile Payments Revolution' (*American Banker*, 29 April 2018), https://www.americanbanker.com/news/why-chinas-mobile-payments-revolution-matters-for-us-bankers.

[24]Vincenzo Bavoso, 'The promise and perils of alternative market-based finance: the case of P2P lending in the UK' (2020) 21(4) Journal of Banking Regulation 395, 401–02.

[25]Rainer Lenz, 'Peer-to-Peer Lending: Opportunities and Risks' (2016) 7 European Journal of Risk Regulation 688, 689–90.

[26]Benjamin Käfer, 'Peer to peer lending: A (financial stability) risk perspective' (2016) MAGKS Joint Discussion Paper Series in Economics, No. 22-2016, 25, http://hdl.handle.net/10419/144687.

investors to design loan portfolios: well-developed P2P platforms (Lending Club, Funding Circle and Prosper)[27] offer automated lending options where a lender can auto-select lending criteria (interest rate, risk profile, market segment).[28] These options improve screening and monitoring services, replacing the chain of intermediation in the assessment of borrowers' creditworthiness and loan requests.[29] This enables the loan application and loan approval processes to be expedited, facilitating timely credit decisions for applicants.[30] Automated lending processes support the human assessment in providing a loan and substantially lower underwriting and compliance costs for lenders; the resulting data can therefore be leveraged to improve their risk management.[31] As a result, software-driven automated decision-making customises the origination and distribution of loans to consumers. However, this is accompanied by the risk of inflating the price of debt securities whilst the lack of transparency and the absence of prudential supervision can affect the quality of the lending market and increase financial instability.[32]

C. Regtech and algorithmic systems

Algorithmic systems expedite the operation of bank intermediaries through sophisticated software which affords the opportunity to analyse legal texts without manual intervention.[33] By employing digital solutions, i.e. a distributed shared ledger, an intermediary can rapidly verify the identity of its clients and assess the potential risks of illegal intentions for the business relationship.[34] Automated decision-making involves information gathering and the communication of prudential risk to investors and regulators, particularly in relation to bank capital rules (e.g. pillar 1 and pillar 2 of Basel II).[35] The use of judgement on the basis of principles rather than mechanical rules is limited in the case of bank capital and applied only for validation of capital models and to capital requirements under pillar 2, reflecting operational and other risks outside the standard categories of market and credit risk (and more recently through adjustments to the conservation buffer of Basel III).[36] Automated systems to calculate risk weights have the potential to make transparent the internal models for credit scoring and loss-absorbency capacity.

Computerised analytical models and centralised standard-setting (e.g. shared data repositories) can create the conditions to aggregate the flows of information and

[27]For an overview of various P2P platforms see Alistair Milne and Paul Parboteeah, 'The Business Models and Economics of Peer-to-Peer Lending' (5 May 2016) ECRI Research Report No 17, https://ssrn.com/abstract=2763682.

[28]Olena Havrylchyk, 'Regulatory framework for the loan-based crowdfunding platforms' (2018) OECD Economics Department Working Papers No. 1513, 13, https://www.oecd-ilibrary.org/content/paper/24ad924a-en.

[29]Kathryn Judge, 'The Future of Direct Finance: The Diverging Paths of Peer-to-Peer Lending and Kickstarter' (2015) 50 Wake Forest Law Review 603, 622–23.

[30]Ding Chen, Anil Savio Kavuri and Alistair Milne, 'Growing Pains: The Changing Regulation of Alternative Lending Platforms' (26 January 2019), 2, https://ssrn.com/abstract=3315738.

[31]W Scott Frame, Larry Wall and Lawrence J White, 'Technological Change and Financial Innovation in Banking: Some Implications for Fintech' (October 2018), Federal Reserve Bank of Atlanta Working Paper 2018-11, 2, https://ssrn.com/abstract=3261732.

[32]Moran Ofir and Ido Sadeh, 'A Revolution in Progress: Regulating P2P Lending Platforms' (17 March 2020), 10, https://ssrn.com/abstract=3530901.

[33]Lawrence Lessing, *Code and Other Laws of Cyberspace* (Basic Books 1999) 43–44.

[34]For an overview, see Kern Alexander, *Principles of Banking Regulation* (CUP 2019) 342.

[35]Douglas W Arner, Janos Barberis and Ross P. Buckey, 'FinTech, RegTech, and the Reconceptualization of Financial Regulation' (2017) 37 Northwestern Journal of International Law & Business 371, 396.

[36]Kenneth A. Bamberger, 'Technologies of Compliance: Risk and Regulation in a Digital Age' (2010) 88 Texas Law Review 669, 731–32.

coordinate more localised regulatory engagements.[37] This centralised approach of risk modelling could redefine the regulatory burden between regulators and banks: advanced predictive analytics can improve the assessment of banks' credit exposure and probability of default.[38] These are applications for AI models which generate predictions with respect to desired outcomes: the decision-making process is based on trained machine learning and underlying computer programmes which give rise to opacity in the data patterns.[39] The development of new data technologies such as blockchain and APIs (Application Programming Interfaces) in the banking industry offers the opportunity, through dialogue between regulators and industry to address this opacity.[40]

Automated methodologies for the modelling and communication of capital at risk are integrated into regulatory frameworks, making the distinction between internal models and standardised approaches meaningless. Automated decision-making could reduce reliance on banks' sources of information about the creditworthiness of borrowers and firms' lending decisions through a shared data platform.[41] This would limit the discretionary review of banks in granting loans while, in parallel, enhancing timely monitoring of risk and the predictability of unexpected losses.

The use of automated methods involves initial cost, risk of error in the system, risk of over-reliance and increased systemic risk if all firms follow similar artificial intelligence solutions that lead to highly homogeneous market behaviour.[42] In this context, recourse to machine learning by bank intermediaries may give rise to certain harms for the credit market. Intelligent systems which make decisions impact humans, and what recourse humans have to take back control when algorithms fail or demonstrate prejudice constitutes a challenge for regulators and policymakers.[43] In such a scenario, most or nearly all financial intermediaries would end up following similar strategies as the algorithms used would be likely to generate herd behaviour effects.[44] Another risk involves the implications of machine disruption for privacy protection and data security. This is evident in the MiFID II algorithmic trading requirements[45] and the widespread industry interest in using a shared third-party for KYC regulations to disclose identity information and hence achieve lower costs of on-boarding.

---

[37]Cristie Ford, 'Prospects for scalability: Relationships and uncertainty in responsive regulation' (2013) 7 Regulation & Governance 14, 24.

[38]Paolo Siciliani, 'The Disruption of the Prudential Regulatory Framework' (2019) 5 Journal of Financial Regulation 220, 233–34.

[39]W Nicholson Price II and Arti K. Rai, 'Clearing Opacity through Machine Learning' (2021) 106(2) Iowa Law Review 775, 784–86.

[40]The experience of the Open Banking initiative in the UK banking sector shows an innovative collaboration between regulators and regulated entities to improve sharing of data among customers with third parties. On this discussion see Nydia Remolina, 'Open Banking: Regulatory Challenges for a New Form of Financial Intermediation in a Data-Driven World' (2019) SMU Centre for AI & Data Governance Research Paper No. 2019/05, 46–47, https://ssrn.com/abstract=3475019.

[41]Ioannis Anagnostopoulos, 'Fintech and regtech: Impact on regulators and banks' (2018) 100 Journal of Economics and Business 7, 14. For a criticism of the use of machine learning in banks, see Larry D Wall, 'Some financial regulatory implications of artificial intelligence' (2018) 100 Journal of Economics and Business 55, 58.

[42]Tom CW Lin, 'Artificial Intelligence, Finance, and the Law' 88 Fordham Law Review 531, 536.

[43]Kristin Johnson, Frank Pasquale and Jennifer Chapman, 'Artificial Intelligence, Machine Learning, and Bias in Finance: Toward Responsible Innovation' (2019) 88 Fordham Law Review 499, 511.

[44]For the herding effect during the 'Flash Crash' see Christian Borch, 'High-frequency trading, algorithmic finance and the Flash Crash: reflections on eventalization' (2016) 45 Economy and Society 350, 364.

[45]See Article 17 of Directive 2014/65/EU of the European Parliament and of the Council of 15 May 2014 on markets in financial instruments and amending Directive 2002/92/EC and Directive 2011/61/EU.

AI models such as deep learning can assist public authorities to expedite the supervisory functions of risk assessment, crisis management and investor protection. For instance, smart contracts and DLT can be used to automate the execution of financial transactions. Code governing a variety of applications could be designed so as to reflect regulatory standards and thus guarantee full compliance.[46] Regtech can support regulators in formulating substantive rules and allow supervisors to assess the impact of a firm's risk models by transferring the underlying data sets into the supervisor's risk model systems.[47]

I. The potential of regtech for firms' operating processes

Regtech is often viewed as a technological response to the vastly increased burden of compliance on financial firms since the global financial crisis.[48] A major part of this increase in regulation has been introduced to enhance the resilience of the financial system, by strengthening prudential rules at the level of both the individual institution and the wider system. There has also been a marked growth in requirements of other forms of regulation, notably conduct of business and also KYC and AML reporting requirements.[49]

The opportunity for making revenues from reducing compliance burdens is an attractive one and has led to a substantial number of regtech start-ups.[50] This is a natural application, with the emergence of new financial technologies running in tandem with the substantial rise in regulatory burden since the crisis.[51] There are however clear limitations to what can be achieved from such automation of compliance. The use of technology in this manner to reduce compliance costs and strengthen supervision can conflict with the exercise of manual or judgmental intervention of regulators, for example in authorisation processes, detection of financial crime, or the identification of mis-selling practices.[52] The technology is often applied to regulatory requirements in the design of financial products in a way that ensures compliance with rules, without the need for human input.[53] In this sense, regtech might be seen as a more 'natural' partner for the rule-based variety of financial regulation, and it is likely that only a relatively small part of the existing

[46]Bart van Liebergen, 'Machine Learning: A Revolution in Risk Management and Compliance?' (2017) 45 Journal of Financial Transformation 60.

[47]Dirk A Zetzsche and others, 'Regulating a Revolution: from Regulatory Sandboxes to Smart Regulation' (2017) 23 Fordham Journal of Corporate & Financial Law 31, 94.

[48]Veerle Colaert, 'Regtech as a Response to Regulatory Expansion in the Financial Sector' (2018) 3 Revue internationale des services financiers/International Journal for Financial Services (RISF) 56.

[49]In the aftermath of the global financial crisis, myriad rules, regulations and guidelines have characterised the KYC and AML framework: the EU Fifth Money Laundering Directive, the FATF principles and MiFID II introduced a greater degree of reporting requirements. See Douglas W Arner, Janos Nathan Barberis and Ross P. Buckley, 'The Emergence of Regtech 2.0: From Know Your Customer to Know Your Data' (2016) 44 Journal of Financial Transformation 79.

[50]A Cambridge Centre for Alternative Finance report Emmanuel Schizas and others, 'The global regtech industry benchmark report' (2019), https://www.jbs.cam.ac.uk/wp-content/uploads/2020/08/2019-12-ccaf-global-regtech-benchmarking-report.pdf, estimates that by early 2019 regtech start-ups worldwide had raised a cumulative $9.7bn of venture capital investment, earned total 2018 revenues of $4.9bn and had 44,000 employees.

[51]Kari Larsen and Shariq Gilani, 'RegTech is the New Black - The Growth of RegTech Demand and Investment' (2017) Journal of Financial Transformation Capco Institute 22.

[52]Mark Carney, 'New Economy, New Finance, New Bank', speech given at The Mansion House, London, 21 June 2018, https://www.bankofengland.co.uk/speech/2018/mark-carney-speech-at-the-lord-mayors-bankers-and-merchants-dinner-mansion-house.

[53]Bank of England and Financial Conduct Authority, 'Machine learning in UK financial services' (October 2019), https://www.bankofengland.co.uk/report/2019/machine-learning-in-uk-financial-services.

financial rulebook can be easily translated into code for use in this manner. Since principles and outcomes remain widely used, this appears to place a fairly substantial limitation on the potential of regtech. It is also conceivable that following on from this, the expanded use of computer code in financial regulation might itself introduce undesirable pressure to shift back to a more command and control-focused regulatory style, raising broader questions about the shift to technology.[54] The potential of regtech is not limited to reduce compliance costs and expedite decision-making processes: it extends to reshape the way customers engage with financial services. Specifically, the regulatory transformations of market infrastructures to include digital identities and blockchain-enabled technologies lead to the use of regtech solutions to foster financial inclusion.[55] Thus, regtech has the potential to support regulators in the supervision of digital payments system in order to maintain financial stability and integrity. In this context, regtech promotes financial inclusion by providing real-time information and data to map financial access and usage to identify gaps in provision.[56] As a result, the employment of regtech to design better financial and regulatory systems to achieve policy objectives facilitates inclusionary services for the underbanked through open access to digital data and wide offer of credit products.[57]

II. The transition to data-driven finance

Modern data technologies have the potential to provide regulatory authorities with near-complete oversight of prudential and conduct risks, both for individual institutions and at the systemic level. One particularly vivid expression of this point of view envisages using technology for the real-time tracking of the global flow of funds.[58] The principal motivation for this broad interpretation of regtech is macroprudential. The global financial crisis strongly reinforced the need for a sufficient degree of system-level oversight to work in addition to the 'microprudential oversight' carried out at the individual-firm level.[59] This suggests a new regime of 'smart' regulation that would harness the transition to data-driven finance in order to allow for something closer to full, real-time oversight, and thereby answer the call of analysts who expressed the desire for such capability in their visions for a safer post-crisis financial system.[60] Hildebrandt argues that smart

[54]On this point, see Katharina Pistor, *The Code of Capital. How the Law Creates Wealth and Inequality* (Princeton University Press 2019) 183–84.

[55]Blockchain-backed regtech supports to create digital identities not only as a regulatory instrument but also to allow market participants to access cross-border financial services. See Soumaya Bhyer and Seyoung Lee, 'Banking the Unbanked and Underbanked: RegTech as an Enabler for Financial Inclusion' in Janos Barberis, Douglas W Arner and Ross P Buckley (eds), *The RegTech Book* (Wiley 2019) 318–19.

[56]Nora Gurung and Leon Perlman, 'Use of Regtech by Central Banks and its Impact on Financial Inclusion' (2018), 46, https://ssrn.com/abstract=3285985. In this context, it is argued that 'the use of regtech to strengthen supervisory capacities of central banks can indirectly impact financial inclusion' (at 50).

[57]Douglas W Arner, and others, 'Sustainability, FinTech and Financial Inclusion' (2020) 21(1) European Business Organization Law Review 7, 16.

[58]Andrew Haldane, 'Managing global finance as a system' (2014) Maxwell Fry Annual Global Finance Lecture at Birmingham University, Bank of England, 9, https://www.bankofengland.co.uk/-/media/boe/files/speech/2014/managing-global-finance-as-a-system.pdf.

[59]Claudio Borio, 'Implementing the macroprudential approach to financial regulation and supervision' in Christopher J Green, Eric J Pentecost and Tom Weyman-Jones (eds), *The Financial Crisis and the Regulation of Finance* (Edward Elgar 2011) 101–02.

[60]Douglas W Arner and others, 'The Future of Data-Driven Finance and RegTech: Lessons from EU Big Bang II' (2020) *25* Stanford Journal of Law, Business & Finance 245, 252.

regulation should identify a code-driven system of cryptographic law capable of taking decisions which affect legal subjects.[61] There are other advocates of this broader interpretation of regtech. Zetzsche and others emphasise the transformative potential of regtech as being where its real 'prize' may lie.[62] Kavassallis and others evidence the potential improvements of risk monitoring where digital standardised documents are made available to all relevant parties, including the supervisory and regulatory authorities.[63] Butler and O'Brien note the transformative potential of such practices for the supervision of the financial system, although greater international harmonisation of regulatory regimes is likely to be required in order fully to harness this wider potential.[64]

A comprehensive market-wide information system in which the regulator sees and responds to every undesired development is not something that is imminently achievable. Rather, the opportunity lies in using technology to improve institutional operations and governance. Technology should be applied to strengthen both management information (making it available, understandable and actionable) and the governance of systems and data within institutions, in order better to achieve both business and regulatory outcomes. This approach to regtech, emphasising its use to facilitate improved data and information availability and hence improve governance and controls, will allow it to be applied to the full range of regulatory operations, not just to the enforcement of reporting and other rules but also to the principle-based approaches that cannot be directly translated into code.

As well as maintaining the present balance in the regulatory regime between rules and principles, this can help avoid other unwanted consequences such as the possibility that increased levels of automated and mechanistic compliance in turn will reduce emphasis on culture and values within financial institutions.[65] This is above all a challenge of governance, for individual firms, for the financial services industry, and for the regulatory authorities. Technology is increasingly central to financial firms, so it is a board responsibility to oversee and ensure effective application of technology in operational and business processes. One challenge is overcoming the divides within firms, between specialists such as those in information technology and data science, and other staff with client facing and operational roles, by 'orchestrating' the adoption of technology so that business understanding and control are maintained. Another challenge is ensuring that senior management and board members have an adequate grasp of both technological opportunities and technological risks.

Achieving the potential of technology requires an unfamiliar degree of co-operation between financial services firms, on data and technology standards, on the sharing of data and on exploring opportunities for shared processing, all pursued with a view to achieving improved long-term outcomes for clients and other stakeholders.[66] This may

---

[61] Mireille Hildebrandt, 'Algorithmic regulation and the rule of law' (2018) 376 Philosophical Transactions of the Royal Society A, 2, https://doi.org/10.1098/rsta.2017.0355.

[62] Dirk A Zetzsche and others, 'From Fintech to Techfin: The Regulatory Challenges of Data-Driven Finance' (2018) 14(2) New York University Journal of Law & Business 393.

[63] Petros Kavassalis and others, 'An innovative RegTech approach to financial risk monitoring and supervisory reporting' (2018) 19 Journal of Risk Finance 39, 39–40.

[64] Tom Butler and Leona O'Brien, 'Understanding regtech for Digital Regulatory Compliance' in Theo Lynn and others (eds), *Disrupting Finance. FinTech and Strategy in the 21st Century* (Palgrave 2019) 85–86.

[65] Karen Yeung, 'Algorithmic regulation: A critical interrogation' (2018) 12 Regulation & Governance 505, 514–15.

[66] Carolyn Abbot, 'Bridging the Gap – Non-state Actors and the Challenges of Regulating New Technology' (2012) 39 Journal of Law and Society 329, 338.

however meet with resistance from managements that have been routinely focused on short-term profit performance. Regulators have a central role going beyond their traditional mandates of oversight from a distance, intervening only when there is an imminent prudential or conduct threat. They will need to take some responsibility for co-ordinating the technological developments and engaging in ongoing dialogue with regulated firms about the most effective means of employing technology to achieve both business and regulatory outcomes.

D. Financial inclusion and digital payments systems

The use of digital payments platforms has exploited the potential of inclusionary services for market participants while increasing the employment of artificial systems to automate decision-making processes. Promises of financial technologies have been lauded in various quarters as advancing both opportunities for regulatory innovation and transaction costs savings.[67] Technology-based payments have become instrumental in promoting small business lending, access to financial services at fair pricing for customers with disabilities and credit for low-income households. The innovation brought about by M-Pesa in Kenya first and then also in Uganda is often cited as integrating unbanked customers to mainstream financial systems.[68] The possibility for technology-centred change in the financial industry is illustrated, for example, by the case of China which has seen rapid shifts to both mobile payments (Alipay, WeChat Pay) largely displacing notes and coins in urban areas; and to non-bank loan intermediation through the dramatic growth in the Chinese version of P2P lending.[69]

The adoption of automated procedures to support manual decisions embeds sophisticated computational techniques driven by algorithms that elaborate the flow of information received from autonomous predictive models. Despite the positive aspects of digital technologies, a growing debate about the data-gathering and the datasets used to elaborate inputs into computerised programmes raises questions about the accuracy of outcomes for final users.[70] The algorithmic codes formulate a series of statements which might reflect the behaviour and routine habits of consumers. However, algorithms may contain biased methodologies inherent because of human error which are apt to amplify undesirable practices, such as the marginalisation and exclusion of protected customers.[71] Further, algorithms are not objective: they do not provide accurate predictions of desired outcomes because they cannot possess the necessary accurate data. As

[67] Irina Mnohoghitnei and others, 'Embracing the Promise of Fintech' (2019) Q1 Bank of England Quarterly Bulletin, 4–5; Douglas W Arner, Janos Barberis and Ross P Buckley, 'The Evolution of FinTech: A New Post-Crisis Paradigm' (2015) 47(4) Georgetown Journal of International Law 1271; Emilios Avgouleas and Aggelos Kiayias, 'The Promise of Blockchain Technology for Global Securities and Derivatives Markets: The New Financial Ecosystem and the 'Holy Grail' of Systemic Risk Containment' (2019) 20(1) European Business Organization Law Review 81, 102–03.

[68] Njuguna Ndung'u, 'The M-Pesa Technological Revolution for Financial Services in Kenya: A Platform for Financial Inclusion' in David Lee, Kuo Chuen and Robert Deng (eds), *Handbook of Blockchain, Digital Finance, and Inclusion, Volume 1: Cryptocurrency, FinTech, InsurTech, and Regulation* (Elsevier 2018) 37–38.

[69] Kieran Garvey and others, 'Cultivating Growth. The 2nd Asia Pacific Region Alternative Finance Industry Report' (September 2017), 57, https://ssrn.com/abstract=3621288.

[70] Jennifer Graham, 'Risk of discrimination in AI systems. Evaluating the effectiveness of current legal safeguards in tackling algorithmic discrimination' in Alison Lui and Nicholas Ryder (eds), *FinTech, Artificial Intelligence and the Law* (Routledge 2021) 215–16.

[71] Lindsay Sain Jones and Goldburn Maynard Jr., 'Unfulfilled Promises of the FinTech Revolution' (2023) 111 California Law Review, forthcoming.

Sunstein argued, 'algorithms may lack information that human beings have, and for that reason, some human beings might be able to outperform algorithms'.[72] Poor training data and discriminatory proxies taint decision-making systems and exploit consumers' behaviour, although it is debated whether the discrimination is intentional or it is a result of mere defective software.[73] Intelligent machines are trained by gathering data which may not necessarily be representative of all classes of consumers considered by the software so as to provide the full range of services. The training data cannot offer a complete reflection of individuals' profiles simply because it is unlikely to incorporate information about inscrutable factual criteria (e.g. financial condition, sexual orientation, level of disability).[74] The reliance on training data has been questioned in terms of poor disclosure and the opaque methods by which the 'black-box' of predictive judgement design is embedded in the internal models.[75] Machine learning analysis can produce wrong assessments of protected categories which replicate manual decisions and lead to the redlining of applicants belonging to the category of disadvantaged customers. Therefore, the quality of financial services available to vulnerable persons is limited in terms of what is on offer on account of constraints affecting the sources of information and unfamiliarity with the operating procedures of artificial systems.[76]

A range of new applications, often based on the transactions data made available through the experience of Open Banking, offers support for savings and decisions[77], along with programmes making automated investment decisions and robo-advisors proffering investment advice.[78] Technology underpins the growth of comparison sites and their use as an alternative to advice from brokers or the media in making saving and investment decisions and is increasingly used in both passive and active investment vehicles. The massification of data and advent of Open Finance create a new environment of inclusionary services for underserved customers.[79] Automated market making and trade execution maintains the net asset value of exchange traded funds against their benchmark and the index tracking of passive mutual funds. A range of active investment funds are increasingly using machine learning and other technology-based decision making in their portfolio allocations alongside management judgements.[80] In this context, new technology-supported asset classes are emerging, including loan-based crowdfunding and crypto asset-based payment systems, such as the 'Libra' initiative launched by Facebook, which operate as crypto stablecoin in smart contract

---

[72]Cass R Sunstein, 'The Use of Algorithms in Society' at 9, https://ssrn.com/abstract=4310137.

[73]Jeremias Adams-Prassl, Reuben Binns and Aislinn Kelly-Lyth, 'Directly Discriminatory Algorithms' (2023) 86(1) Modern Law Review 144, 148–49.

[74]Christine Riefa, 'Protecting Vulnerable Consumers in the Digital Single Market' (2022) 33(4) European Business Law Review 607, 612–13.

[75]Kimberly A Houser, 'Can AI Solve the Diversity Problem in the Tech Industry: Mitigating Noise and Bias in Employment Decision-Making' (2019) 22(2) Stanford Technology Law Review 290, 341–43.

[76]Peter Cartwright, 'Understanding and Protecting Vulnerable Financial Consumers' (2015) 38(2) Journal of Consumer Policy 119, 120–21.

[77]Markos Zachariadis and Pinar Ozcan, 'The API Economy and Digital Transformation in Financial Services: The Case of Open Banking' (2017) SWIFT Institute Working Paper No. 2016-001, https://ssrn.com/abstract=2975199.

[78]Tom Baker and Benedict Dellaert, 'Regulating Robo Advice across the Financial Services Industry' (2017) 103(2) Iowa Law Review 713, 728–30.

[79]Francesco De Pascalis, 'The Journey to Open Finance: Learning from the Open Banking Movement' (2022) 33(3) European Business Law Review 397, 401–02.

[80]Reinhard Steennot, 'Robo-advisory services and investor protection' (2021) 3/4 Law and Financial Markets Review forthcoming.

platforms.[81] Cryptoassets have the potential to overcome the current barriers of decentralised blockchain networks but constitute a challenge to policymakers, regulators and stakeholders because of the risk of altering the money market.[82] They operate outside the central banks' arena, bringing an innovative mechanism of lending and free money transfers: this would certainly be a new frontier for cross-border payment systems.[83] In this context, open banking and regtech relate to decentralised provision of financial services which employs technology to provide market participants access and control of the data. As Zetzsche and others argued, 'financial inclusion [...] comes from the decentralization of finance enabling the embedding of local compliance standards and customs which tend to reduce costs of access to financial services'.[84] Decentralized Finance (DeFI) has the potential to reduce intermediary costs, increase transparency through blockchain-based records, provide round-the-clock access to financial markets, expedite settlement transactions, and increase financial inclusion by allowing anyone globally with an internet connection to access DeFi platforms.[85] For example, cryptoassets could have significant potential inclusionary services for remittances by foreign workers which are subject to excessive transfer fees and use obsolete technology.[86] Using technology to enable speedy transfer of remittances at nearly zero costs (including as a major innovation FX conversion) in an environment that is safe from external threats can have an appreciable impact on financial inclusion, especially where remittances are an important part of a family's annual income.[87] Through the use of digital ID and other identification techniques it can secure access to the unbanked giving the opportunity to keep the bulk of the remittances in safe storage. Currently, remittances by migrant workers are subject to high transfer fees. Whether a social media company such as Facebook – whose leadership has identified the need for efficiency in cross-border transfers and retail remittances – can improve the lives of migrant workers and the families that those workers support back in their home countries is an open question.[88]

Safe storage of savings emanating from the remittances, once a part of them has gone into consumption, gives poor households and the previously unbanked the possibility to receive stable and predictable returns on savings, which would allow for better planning of the households' consumption and investment needs. Then, the transfer of some of the balances into a savings account would allow the very poor and the unbanked to use some of the funds to buy insurance to cover the impact on earnings of health and other

[81] Libra can rely on a platform of nearly 2.5 billion Facebook users and aims to have reserve backing and regulatory approval. For an overview of the potential of cryptocurrencies see Edmund Schuster, 'Cloud Crypto Land' (2021) 84 (5) Modern Law Review 974, 984–85.

[82] Michael Anderson Schillig, ''Lex Cryptographi(c)a,' 'Cloud Crypto Land' or What? – Blockchain Technology on the Legal Hype Cycle' (2023) 86(1) Modern Law Review 31, 49–50.

[83] Nydia Remolina, 'The Regulatory and Legal Issues of Decentralized Finance' (2023) Singapore Management University School of Law Research Paper, https://papers.ssrn.com/sol3/papers.cfm?abstract_id=4243544.

[84] Dirk A Zetzsche, Douglas W Arner and Ross P Buckley, 'Decentralized Finance' (2020) 6(2) Journal of Financial Regulation 172, 184.

[85] Steven L Schwarcz and Robert Bourret, 'Fractionalizing Investment Securities: Using FinTech to Expand Financial Inclusion' (2023) 84(1) Ohio State Law Journal, forthcoming.

[86] Whether a social media company such as Facebook – whose leadership has clearly identified the need for efficiency in cross-border transfers and remittances in particular for individuals and SMEs – can improve the lives of foreign workers and the families that those workers support back in their home countries is an open question. On this discussion, see Kavita Datta, ''Mainstreaming' the 'Alternative'? The Financialization of Transnational Migrant Remittances' in Ron Martin and Jane Pollard (eds), *Handbook on the Geographies of Money and Finance* (Edward Elgar 2017) 539–40.

[87] Marc Pilkington, 'Blockchain Technology: Principles and Applications' in F Xavier Olleros and Majlinda Zhegu (eds), *Research Handbook on Digital Transformations* (Edward Elgar 2016) 225–26.

[88] Kavita Datta, *Migrants and their Money: Surviving Financial Exclusion in London* (The Policy Press 2012) 141–42.

contingencies (e.g. a bad harvest). Moreover, turning part of the remittances into savings in a seamless process constrains consumption for instant gratification and can boost the long-term investment plans of low-income households.[89] Further, carefully planned savings balances may eventually be used for the purpose of human capital development including private investment on education. Finally, cash balances can be used as collateral to enable very poor households and the previously unbanked to acquire capital assets such as machinery, which can boost the productivity and income of a small business. However, a number of issues related to financial stability, privacy considerations and compliance with money laundering and countering the financing of terrorism rules remains a potential stumbling block for DeFI platforms.[90]

Financial services firms are increasingly automating credit and insurance risk assessment, fraud detection, and other financial services processes. There is a shift from more mechanical rules to algorithms that utilise a wide range of data sources ('big data') and software that can update itself and learn from its own performance; this is one definition of artificial intelligence, software that learns from data rather than having all rules pre-programmed.[91] Automated tools are increasingly used in credit scoring and in loan and insurance origination, substantially lowering costs and offering potential improvements in risk measurement and management.[92] These technological innovations prompt questions about oversight and transparency.[93]

Notable episodes of undesired outcomes of algorithmic systems are found in the biased pricing of credit or insurance products, based not on actual risk of loss but other customer characteristics such as age, religion or ethnicity.[94] Discriminatory results of sophisticated algorithms employed to assess the creditworthiness of customers led to evident bias against 'people of colour' in the widely used Fair Isaac Corporation (FICO) credit scoring in the United States, perpetuating a dual credit system.[95] The key question is therefore not whether a new technology is biased or not (all processes contain some bias), but rather ensuring it is adopted in a way that is consistent with desired regulatory outcomes. The adoption of any new technologies should therefore be expected to reduce bias, alongside improvements in process efficiency.[96] This should not only be articulated as a regulatory principle, but also supported by dialogue between regulators and industry; in the case of FICO, it should explore the development of a more sophisticated credit scoring assessment more accurately reflecting default risk, with less bias.[97]

---

[89] Friederike Rühmann and others, 'Can blockchain technology reduce the cost of remittances?' (April 2020) OECD Development Co-operation Working Papers, No 73, 16–17.

[90] Igor Makarov and Antoinette Schoar, 'Cryptocurrencies and Decentralized Finance (DEFI)' (2022) NBER Working Paper 30006, 27–28, http://www.nber.org/papers/w30006.

[91] Yavar Bathaee, 'The Artificial Intelligence Black Box and the Failure of Intent and Causation' (2018) 31 Harvard Journal of Law & Technology 890, 898–99.

[92] W Scott Frame, Larry Wall and Lawrence J White, 'Technological Change and Financial Innovation in Banking: Some Implications for fintech' (October 2018), Federal Reserve Bank of Atlanta Working Paper 2018-11, 2.

[93] Tal Zarsky, 'The Trouble with Algorithmic Decisions: An Analytic Road Map to Examine Efficiency and Fairness in Automated and Opaque Decision Making' (2016) 41 Science, Technology, & Human Values 118, 122–23.

[94] Tal Z Zarsky, 'Transparent Predictions' (2013) 2013 University of Illinois Law Review 1503, 1549.

[95] Lisa Rice and Deidre Swesnik, 'Discriminatory effects of credit scoring on communities of color' (2013) 46 Suffolk University Law Review 935, 966.

[96] Aaron Klein, 'Reducing bias in AI-based financial services' (2020) AI Governance Series, Brookings Institute, https://www.brookings.edu/research/reducing-bias-in-ai-based-financial-services/. See also Caroline Conway, 'Fico's dominance in US credit scoring under challenge' (*Financial Times*, 22 June 2021), https://www.ft.com/content/046dd89d-7047-4ed4-af31-0e126f59eb00.

[97] Alex Gano, 'Disparate Impact and Mortgage Lending: A Beginner's Guide' (2017) 88 University of Colorado Law Review 1109, 1167. For example, one source of racial bias in FICO is its 30% weight on mortgage and other credit repayment

Another significant example of undesired outcomes of automated decision-making process is found in the UK Post Office scandal, a case of faulty accounting software which caused reporting shortfalls and resulted in postmasters being wrongly convicted as a result of computer errors.[98] The Post Office's sophisticated IT system, the Horizon software, was at the epicentre of false statements about incorrect missing money from branch accounts.[99] Defective data used to feed cloud-based machines produced inaccurate information about the financial profile of employees. Poor management decisions and failures of investigation and disclosure were involved, calling in question the reliability of technology products and a big tech company supplier.[100] This also evidenced a lack of monitoring of the dataset and predictive models, which employed flawed variables elaborated in the software.[101] The transparency and the fairness of the computer methodologies are the crux of the matter for the quality of the output. Trustworthy in mechanical instruments may hide practices that are designed (intentionally or in self-interested unfamiliarity) to perpetuate biased procedures: the experience of the British Post Office revealed an inherent dependency on the vulnerability of automated programmes.[102]

The potential benefits of digital payments system should be weighed carefully against the risks.[103] In the long term, there is scope for AI to be used as a service-provider for network interconnectedness and as a tool to monitor the business conduct of financial institutions.[104] Although machines can be more reliable than humans, new risks can be built into systems. The question arises as to whether the use of AI automatically excludes certain classes of consumers.[105] The risk of discrimination is also associated with the disruption of computer programmes, which cause lack of transparency and unfair practices.[106] Weaknesses in managing and interpreting the amount of data provided by machines constitute a barrier to the application of AI in the financial sector.

---

history; with no weight on rent repayment history, biasing against renters including many people of colour. An amendment of FICO with a supporting record of rental repayment data, while clearly challenging, would reduce bias.

[98]Nick Wallis, *The Great Post Office Scandal* (Bath Publishing 2021). See also Ian Lloyd, 'Lessons on Robustness and Reliability of Software Solutions from the Horizon System for UK Post Offices' (2022) 23(1) Computer Law Review International at 6–7.

[99]Camilla Cavendish, 'Britain's Post Office scandal claimed hundreds of victims, but what of its villains?' (*Financial Times*, 18 February 2022), https://www.ft.com/content/315f7a16-1549-4558-8520-27621bd9132a.

[100]Jeremy Weinstein, Rob Reich and Mehran Sahami, *System Error: Where Big Tech Went Wrong and How We Can Reboot* (Hachette 2021) ch3.

[101]Rory Cellan-Jones, 'The Great Post Office Scandal — a shameful story of justice denied' (*Financial Times*, 9 December 2021), https://www.ft.com/content/77a3b8cd-26f1-4328-b226-84200fc14808.

[102]Alexander Hicks, 'Transparency, Compliance, And Contestability When Code Is(n't) Law' in NSPW '22: New Security Paradigms Workshop, 24–27 October 2022, New Hampshire, USA, https://arxiv.org/pdf/2205.03925v2.pdf. See also Archie Drake and others, 'Legal contestation of artificial intelligence-related decision-making in the United Kingdom: reflections for policy' (2022) 36(2) International Review of Law, Computers & Technology 251, 271–72.

[103]Cristie Ford, *Innovation and the State: Finance, Regulation, and Justice* (CUP 2017) 152–53. See also Iris HY Chiu, 'A Rational Regulatory Strategy for Governing Financial Innovation' (2017) 8(4) European Journal of Risk Regulation 743.

[104]Marshall W Van Alstyne, Geoffrey G Parker and Sangeet Paul Choudary, 'Pipelines, Platforms, and the New Rules of Strategy' (April 2016) 94 Harvard Business Review at 54–55.

[105]Amit Datta, Michael Carl Tschantz and Anupam Datta, 'Automated Experiments on Ad Privacy Settings. A Tale of Opacity, Choice, and Discrimination' (2015) 1 Proceedings on Privacy Enhancing Technologies 92. See also Izabella Kaminska, 'Algorithmic discrimination' (*Financial Times*, 29 November 2016), https://ftalphaville.ft.com/2016/11/29/2180424/algorithmic-discrimination/.

[106]Matthew U Scherer, 'Regulating Artificial Intelligence Systems: Risks, Challenges, Competencies, and Strategies' (2016) 29 Harvard Journal of Law & Technology 353, 359.

E. Conclusion

The range of digital technologies used in financial services is very broad, including household and small business lending, online and mobile payments, insurance, capital market transactions, wealth management and regulatory reporting and compliance. Likewise, a wide range of digital initiatives seek to promote financial inclusion. With the advent of digital payments systems, lenders have the possibility to access more information in order to assess the credit quality of borrowers and to make decisions on whether (and how much) to lend more quickly. Promoting technological innovation through alternatives to credit means integrating vulnerable and excluded customers into mainstream financial systems.

The use of algorithms and computer systems to coordinate supervisory authorities has become a key component in facilitating the delivery of transactions and improving firm's operational processes, although it can pose risks of undesired biases.[107] In this context, regtech can facilitate compliance processes, while ensuring information disclosure and contractual certainty and predictability of enforcement actions in order to avoid poor outcomes for customers.[108] The 'narrow' interpretation of regtech seeks to automate compliance and hence reduce its costs; while the broad interpretation presents an ambitious vision of comprehensive regulatory oversight that anticipates and prevents undesired outcomes. The central challenge of regtech is not simply 'automated regulation', but rather establishing the appropriate governance of technology in financial services, involving regulators, regulated firms, and technology suppliers.

Regulators employ technology to monitor compliance requirements and prevent suspicious activities (e.g. cybercrime, money laundering, fraudulent transactions). However, the adoption of intelligent machines raises concerns about the appropriateness of supervisory authorities' policies to ensure that making data machine-readable entails accurate control and permissioning for access to and use of data which can reduce regulatory burdens and transaction costs.[109]

An automated decision-making process can enhance the governance of data: it encompasses risk management and minimises reputational risk, legal risk and operational risk.[110] Furthermore, automated procedures can expedite real-time information, particularly with respect to the asset quality of banks' balance sheets (automatic credit scoring) and for compliance with rules on conduct (e.g. mis-selling or rogue trading).[111] Automated practices such as sandboxes experiment with fintech products through natural language processing and cognitive computing in order to secure compliance with regulatory process and supervision.[112]

---

[107]On this point see an interesting editorial of Gillian Tett, 'Artificial intelligence is reshaping finance' (*Financial Times*, 19 November 2020), https://www.ft.com/content/c7d9a81c-e6a3-4f37-bbfd-71dcefda3739.

[108]Douglas W. Arner, Ross P. Buckley and Janos Barberis, 'A FinTech and RegTech Overview: Where We Have Come From and Where We Are Going' in Arner, Buckley and Barberis (n 5) vi.

[109]Jay P Kesan, Carol M Hayes and Masooda N Bashir, 'Information Privacy and Data Control in Cloud Computing: Consumers, Privacy Preferences, and Market Efficiency' (2013) 70 Washington & Lee Law Review 341, 365. It is argued that 'machine learning is the process of training a computational model to accomplish a task with data'. See also John Nay, 'Natural Language Processing and Machine Learning for Law and Policy Texts' (7 April 2018), https://ssrn.com/abstract=3438276.

[110]Alison Lui and George William Lamb, 'Artificial intelligence and augmented intelligence collaboration: regaining trust and confidence in the financial sector' (2018) 27 Information & Communications Technology Law 267, 268–69.

[111]Christine Lagarde, 'Central Banking and FinTech. A Brave New World' (2018) 12 Innovations: Technology, Governance, Globalization 4, 6.

[112]Hilary J Allen, 'Regulatory Sandboxes' (2019) 87 George Washington Law Review 579, 582–83.

Technological applications in banking services have attracted much attention from stakeholders and regulators, both because of the perception that they should support domestic capacity in what is a nascent and rapidly growing new industry with potential global impact, and because digital technology can address some of the perceived shortcomings of the traditional financial services industry (e.g. lack of consumer protection, weaknesses in governance, gaps in compliance and improved provision to previously underserved regions). The UK Government has launched a Fintech Sector strategy, which includes the formation of a 'Cryptoassets Taskforce' with the aim of positioning the UK at the forefront of harnessing the potential benefits of the underlying technology, while guarding against potential risks.[113] Supervisory authorities are also taking steps to support innovation with a leading role played by 'Project Innovate' and regulatory sandboxes programmes at the FCA, which allow automated machines to reduce the manual intervention of regulators.[114] Banks are adapting to this innovation and technology offers opportunities and risks to payment intermediation.

The alternative provision of payments promotes financial inclusion globally, widening access to banking and insurance services both for vulnerable households and small businesses. However, financial services innovation (cryptographic security, massive data processing, distributed computing, artificial intelligence) and new software solutions for delivering financial services (crowdfunding platforms, cryptocurrencies, blockchain) require constant dialogue between regulators and regulated institutions on the appropriate design of regulation and its technological implementation. This dialogue needs to align itself with the ongoing widespread digital transformation of the operational processes, business organisation and market structure across technology products. The increasing mainstreaming of the cryptoasset industry provides customers access to decentralised forms of finance, particularly in relation to remittances, although it has the potential to alter the global payments system while, in turn, potentially leading to market disruption.

Acknowledgement

The author wishes to thank the conference organisers, Colin King and Saskia Hufnagel, and panel participants for their stimulating conversations and insightful thoughts upon the presentation of a draft of this article. Any errors or omissions remain the sole responsibility of the author. The author is grateful to the anonymous reviewers for the useful comments provided on an early draft.

Disclosure statement

No potential conflict of interest was reported by the author(s).

ORCID

Andrea Miglionico http://orcid.org/0000-0002-2114-6709

[113]HM Treasury-Financial Conduct Authority-Bank of England, 'Cryptoassets Taskforce: final report' (October 2018), https://www.gov.uk/government/publications/cryptoassets-taskforce.

[114]FCA, 'The Impact and Effectiveness of Innovate' (April 2019), https://www.fca.org.uk/publications/research/impact-and-effectiveness-innovate.

Crypto payments – a danger to consumer protection?

Louise Damkjær Christensen

ABSTRACT
The original intended function of bitcoin was as a means of payment, but this has turned out to be just one utility of the underlying technology – cryptography. This article goes back to the initial purpose, the means of payment in cryptocurrencies, and examines the problems arising for consumers when paying in crypto. Problems covering execution of payments, liability and the missing issuer of cryptocurrencies, and the volatility of cryptocurrencies and inherent systemic risks will be examined in relation to the MiCA Regulation. This enables a discussion on possible regulatory solutions to protect consumers paying with cryptocurrencies. The paper concludes that the MiCA Regulation does not sufficiently protect consumers in this aspect but proposes an alternative solution to secure appropriate levels of consumer protection.

A. Introduction

While the 2nd Payment Services Directive 2015/2366 (PSD2[1]) ensures appropriate consumer protection for payments covered under its scope, payments in unbacked crypto-assets, also known as cryptocurrencies,[2] are not covered by the same protective measures. Payments in cryptocurrencies are an increasing phenomenon among consumers which calls for further examination of the legal position of consumers paying for goods with cryptocurrencies.[3]

When unbacked crypto-assets are used as a means of payment, a number of issues present themselves. These pose a threat to consumer protection which regulation might be best suited to address. From a consumer-perspective, the most concerning

[1]Directive (EU) 2015/2366 of the European Parliament and of the Council of 25 November 2015 on payment services in the internal market.

[2]While the literature generally refers to this class of crypto-assets as cryptocurrencies the MiCA Regulation 2023/1114 reduces this class to unbacked crypto-assets by establishing a clear line between these and e-money tokens and asset-backed crypto-assets. In this article the terms unbacked crypto-assets and cryptocurrencies will be used interchangeably.

[3]UC Cabuk and M Silenzi, 'Cryptocurrencies in Retail: Consumer Adoption Report 2022' (2022) shows an increase in crypto-consumers from 2021 to 2022; C Baker and K Werbach, 'Blockchain in Financial Services' in J Madir (ed), *FinTech – Law and Regulation* (Edward Elgar 2019) 136 report industry participants to be keen on investing in the payment solution; Deloitte, 'Merchants Getting Ready for Crypto – Merchant Adoption of Digital Currency Payments Survey' (2022) reports on merchants expecting to accept crypto payments within two years; and M Rimol, 'Gartner 2019 Hype Cycle for Blockchain Business Shows Blockchain Will Have a Transformational Impact Across Industries in Five to 10 Years' (2019) reports continuous uptake and progress in the crypto industry.

issue is the one of unbacked crypto-assets' volatility.[4] The unstable value of unbacked crypto-assets makes it difficult for consumers to use them for purchasing goods as their value, and hence the price for goods, vary to an extent that is too complex for the average consumer to manage. Another issue is the difference in regulatory treatment between 'traditional' payments and crypto payments, which poses a potential systemic risk. The question here is whether payments in cryptocurrencies truly call for different regulation when considering the shared function. The last issue treated in this article, is the problem of certainty in execution of initiated payments and potential liability for wrongful or missing execution. It is of vital importance that consumers can trust the finality of payments when transacting and that transactions can be stopped or has a right of recourse in cases of fraud.

The Markets in Crypto-Assets Regulation (MiCAR) aims to create legal certainty, enhance financial stability, and promote innovation and the use of crypto-assets by enhancing the protection of consumers and investors.[5] Particularly the claim to be enhancing consumer protection is interesting in relation to the above-mentioned threats surrounding payments in cryptocurrencies. This article accounts for these threats to consumer protection and examines whether the MiCAR addresses these in line with the prescribed goals of enhancing consumer protection and creating legal certainty.[6]

The presented threats will be further described in Section B, which focuses on the relevant considerations regarding consumers connected to each problem. Section C will examine whether the MiCAR manages to address the issues presented with an inquiry into relevant provisions. Based on these findings, Section D will discuss potential solutions to address the threats to consumer protection enabling a safe regulatory framework for payments in unbacked crypto-assets. Finally, Section E will conclude on the findings of the article.

B. The threats to consumer protection

Consumers, as a group, are considered to be troubled by individual, biased decision-making, causing them difficulties in, not only obtaining, but also understanding and processing necessary information for making financial decisions.[7] Furthermore, reports continue to show that consumers also on average possess low financial literacy, making financial decision-making troublesome.[8]

The world of crypto-assets has generally caused trouble for regulators when trying to create suitable regulatory frameworks. The increase in adoption of payments in unbacked

[4]MA Schillig, 'Cryptocurrencies: Development and Perspectives' in I Chiu and G Deipenbrock (eds), *Routledge Handbook of Financial Technology and Law* (Routledge 2021) 333, also see J Son, M Huseyin Bilgin and D Ryu, 'Consumer Choices Under New Payment Methods' (2022) 82 Financial Innovation 4.

[5]Regulation (EU) 2023/1114 of the European Parliament and of the Council of 31 May 2023 on markets in crypto-assets, recitals 5 and 6.

[6]That is, crypto-for-crypto and crypto-for-fiat currency exchanges are not covered by the scope of this paper which only covers crypto-for-goods transactions.

[7]Also see J Armour and others, *Principles of Financial Regulation* (Oxford University Press 2016) 60.

[8]European Banking Authority, 'EBA Financial Education Report 2019/2020' (2020) documents a lower than expected literacy as well as insufficient financial education provided by NCAs, Financial Conduct Authority, 'Research Note: Cryptoasset Consumer Research 2021' shows a group of crypto consumers mistakenly believing they have the same protection paying in crypto as when paying in fiat currencies, and Cabuk and Silenzi (n 3) section 6 document a not insignificant number of crypto consumers holding cryptocurrencies as a last resort to enable payments. As such, there is not always a difference in the level of sophistication between crypto consumers and consumers in general.

crypto-assets among consumers calls for special attention to the specific issues related hereto.[9] Before delving further into these, it is necessary to describe what a payment transaction in cryptocurrency looks like and to outline key differences between cryptocurrencies and fiat currencies as means of payment.

1. The crypto payment transaction

Broadly speaking, crypto payments can be configured in two ways – with de jure intermediaries or with de facto intermediaries. The latter option is also the original version without traditional intermediaries as intended by the founding father of cryptocurrencies.[10] Here, the payer programmed the transaction on their computer, leaving it to the miners to verify the transaction and update the ledger (as illustrated in Figure 1).

The term 'de facto' intermediaries are used for this option, as the miners are de facto intermediaries necessary to complete the payment transaction.[11] Although developments in the crypto-asset services have provided for custodial wallet services, which are not dependent on the miners, non-custodial wallets still exist and depend on this traditional effort provided by miners.

Developments in the crypto economy have led to an increasing number of payment gateways or services through which crypto payments have become more accessible to ordinary consumers. For the purchase of goods, in-store or online, merchants can choose to use a gateway, or payment service, for accepting payments in cryptocurrency. With such a gateway the payer can use a mobile wallet app to pay for the goods, and the merchant receives the payment from the service provider once it has been processed and fees have been credited the amount (as illustrated in Figure 2).[12] The primary downside of this innovation in crypto payments is the fact that such a de jure intermediary is in direct opposition to the original purpose of creating cryptocurrencies which sought to eliminate intermediaries.[13]

Comparing paying in unbacked crypto-assets to fiat currency, the most characteristic difference is the fact that fiat currencies hold (national) legal tender and are issued by central banks.[14] Other important characteristics are that fiat currencies are considered units of account, recognised as a medium of exchange, and are perceived to store value.[15]

Despite these differences, unbacked crypto-assets can be used as a means of payment when the parties to a contract of sale or exchange agree to be paid in a chosen cryptocurrency. As such, cryptocurrencies can be considered as units of value between the parties to a contract, agreeing that these units of value fulfil the monetary function

---

[9]According to Baker and Werbach (n 3) 136, industry participants are also highly interested in investing in blockchain-based solutions in the payments area.

[10]In particular, of course, the bitcoin as described by S Nakamoto, 'Bitcoin: A Peer-to-Peer Electronic Cash System' (2008).

[11]As recital 22 MiCAR also establishes, these de facto intermediaries are not covered by the scope of the MiCAR.

[12]It is for the individual merchant to decide whether they receive cryptocurrencies or if the payer's cryptocurrency will be transferred into a fiat currency or a different cryptocurrency. The merchant pays the fees to the service provider, but of course, this does not prevent the merchant from charging the payer a transaction fee, which further highlights the consumer protection-related issues of crypto payments.

[13]Nakamoto (n 10).

[14]H de Vauplane, 'Cryptocurrencies and Central Banks' in Madir (n 3) 112.

[15]ibid 113 and C Harwick, 'Cryptocurrency and the Problem of Intermediation' (2016) 20 The Independent Review 569, 573.

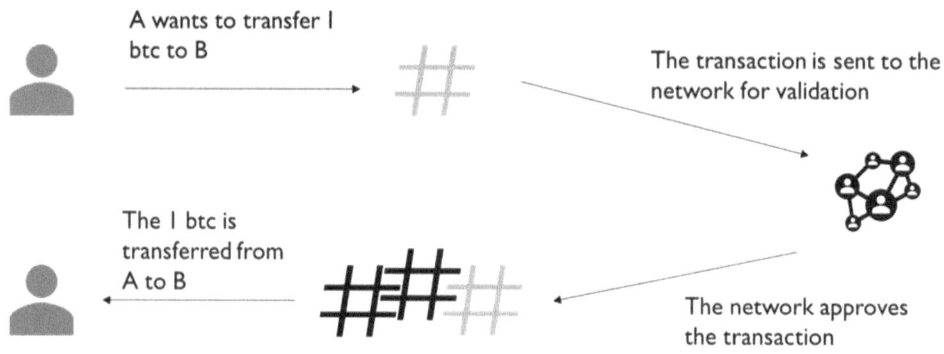

Figure 1. Transaction with non-custodial wallet.

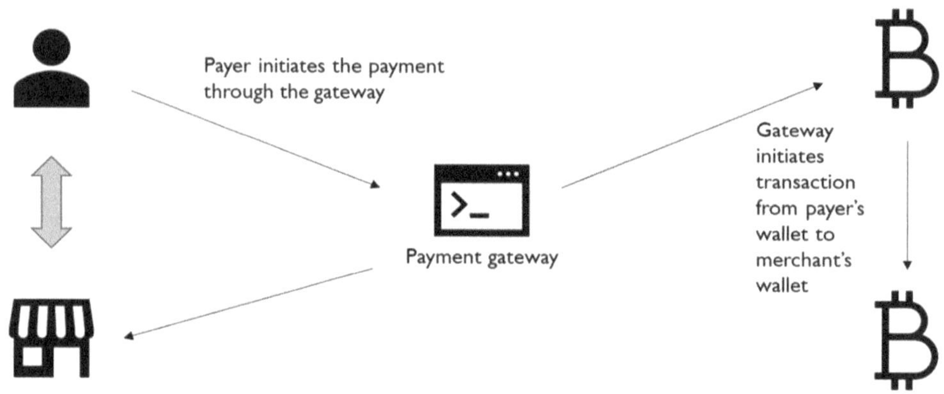

Figure 2. Transaction with custodial wallet.

usually applied to fiat currencies.[16] Such an agreement, though, can cause problems to arise which could pose a considerable danger to consumer protection. The following subsections will describe some of the threats which hold particular issues regarding consumer protection. The threats treated are the volatility of unbacked crypto-assets, their inherent systemic risk, and the issues related to execution and liability.

2. The volatility of unbacked crypto-assets

The duality of unbacked crypto-assets' function, being used as both a means of exchange or payment and as an investment, has since the dawn of bitcoin caused volatility in the value of unbacked crypto-assets. This was particularly evident with the great fluctuations during 2022,[17] and the even more recent crash of the FTX trading platform only adds to the concerns surrounding crypto.[18]

Taking a closer look at cryptocurrencies' function, two different classifications are possible. The first classification is the one treated at present, as a means of payment, while the

[16]Vauplane (n 14) 114 and Harwick (n 15) 573 who also refer to Ludwig von Mises' regression theorem stating that somthing is money when people use it as money.
[17]European Securities and Markets Authority, 'Crypto-Assets and Their Risks for Financial Stability' (2022) 3.
[18]A Herman, 'Will the FTX Crash Kill Crypto?' (*Forbes*, 14 December 2022) <https://www.forbes.com/sites/arthurherman/2022/12/14/will-the-ftx-crash-kill-crypto/?sh=6088e52421f3> (accessed 31 January 2023).

second option is as an investment. There is nothing new in currency holding these two functions at the same time, as foreign currency exchange trading (FX trading) is a well-known option to diversify an investor's portfolio.[19] Where the case of cryptocurrencies differs from traditional, fiat currency FX trading is, in particular, regarding the volatility of the value of cryptocurrencies. While unbacked crypto-assets are not pegged to any asset or fiat currency, but rely on demand and supply, they are inherently unstable, whereas many fiat currencies, despite FX trading, maintain stable value. Another issue is the preference among users to hold these unbacked crypto-assets as investments. With crypto-assets lacking inherent value, the volatility becomes more acute than is the case for fiat currencies, especially for less sophisticated investors such as consumers.[20]

The volatility of cryptocurrencies is also the primary reason for its inability to be units of account in a stable manner.[21] Furthermore, as a means of payment, the price volatility makes unbacked crypto-assets less effective as it causes difficulty for both payer and payee to establish the currency's value in exchange for the good which value is already settled in a fiat currency. Finally, the volatile growth cycles linked to crypto-assets entail risks which could in the future pose a threat to not only consumers but also financial stability if the crypto economy continues to grow excessively.[22] As the market for crypto-assets has been unable to manage the excessive volatility of unbacked crypto-assets, it is worth examining whether regulation can contribute to a safer solution for consumers paying in cryptocurrencies.

3. *Systemic risks and crypto payments*

With the crypto-economy effectively consisting of a crypto-class of unbacked crypto-assets, which are being used predominantly as a means of payment, the differential treatment in applicable regulatory framework causes systemic risks to increase as the payment method fluctuates in popularity.[23] The function of this class of crypto-assets is the same as that of fiat currencies, or in terms of the PSD2, as funds.[24] Although the function of the subject is the same, the regulation covering it is not. Payments using 'funds' are covered by the PSD2 whereas payments in cryptocurrencies will soon become covered by the MiCAR but have so far been unregulated.

Placing payments in unbacked crypto-assets outside a regulatory framework creates the opportunity for providers in the unregulated space to provide second-grade service though without the consumers necessarily being aware of the different regulatory requirements. This increases the threat to financial stability, and especially the financial markets' integrity, though it seems to be sought covered by adopting the MiCAR. But providing different regulatory regimes for the same function could potentially cause systemic risks to the payments market, resulting in market fragmentation and an unlevel playing

[19] Vauplane (n 14) 114 also compares cryptocurrencies to FX trading when dealing with volatility and inflationary risk.
[20] Also see European Securities and Markets Authority (n 17) 9, L Hermans and others, 'Decrypting Financial Stability Risks in Crypto-Asset Markets' (2022) Financial Stability Review and I Chiu, *Regulating the Crypto Economy: Business Transformations and Financialisation* (Hart 2021) 209.
[21] Vauplane (n 14) and Son, Bilgin and Ryu (n 4) 4.
[22] Also see the conclusion in European Securities and Markets Authority (n 17) 14.
[23] Although the current situation is found to be manageable by ESMA, see ibid.
[24] PSD2, art 4(1)(25).

field for payment services across the EU.[25] This problem was also present prior to the adoption of PSD2, where the regime in PSD1 did not cover third-party payment service providers causing the group to remain mostly unregulated. The primary differences between that case, of the unregulated third-party payment service providers, and this case, with payments in unbacked crypto-assets, are three-fold. The first difference is the technology applied to provide not only the payment service, but also the unit of exchange – the pathology of cryptographic technology. The second difference is the lack of legal recognition of cryptocurrencies as being (nationally) legal tender and to classify it with monetary value. The third and last difference is the missing intermediaries.

Leaving a payment function either unregulated, or covered by a different regulatory framework, is unsustainable for the EU's aim to create an internal market. The different regulations also conflict with the Union's goal of competitive markets and the objective of ensuring a level playing-field. The threat it poses to consumer protection also carries great weight when justifying regulatory intervention to deal with the potential systemic risks. Though, it is first necessary to examine to which degree the MiCAR increases, or decreases, consumer protection on this aspect.

4. Lack of accountability and liability

A cherished trait of crypto-assets in the crypto-community is the lack of intermediaries.[26] Once crypto-assets, or cryptocurrencies, have been issued, there is neither accountability nor liability concerns for the issuer of the tokens. As such, a trait of the crypto-economy is that holders of cryptocurrencies have no claim against the issuer. This means that the issuer of an unbacked crypto-asset cannot be held accountable nor liable for losses incurred by the holders, effectively leaving consumers holding these assets to bear all losses personally. Adding to the problem is the low financial literacy among consumers, and their biased, individual decision-making.[27] Being considered less able to collect and process necessary information, the threat poses an even greater problem. The graveness of this situation is further stressed by the fact that issuers and service providers have no obligations to disclose this information – the lack of accountability and liability – to users of cryptocurrencies.[28]

With cryptocurrency transactions all transaction initiations are finite even before execution is completed. This is the case even when the wrong payee has been added to the order, if the amount was denominated mistakenly, or if the private key has been stolen and the transaction is fraudulent. In all these cases, the payer is liable for all loses personally.[29] This stands in stark contrast to the protective measures of arts 71–74 PSD2, which protect consumers from, particularly, fraudulent or incorrect transactions. To leave consumers without this protection when paying in cryptocurrencies

[25] European Commission, 'Commission Staff Working Document Impact Assessment Accompanying the document Proposal for a Regulation of the European Parliament and of the Council on Markets in Crypto-assets and amending Directive (EU) 2019/1937' SWD(2020) 380 final 2020, 11.

[26] Also see Baker and Werbach (n 3) 129.

[27] European Banking Authority, 'EBA Financial Education Report 2019/2020' scores EU citizens to have a low financial literacy score on average.

[28] Financial Conduct Authority (n 8) found that a not insignificant number of consumers holding crypto-assets thought there were legal protection connected to their holdings.

[29] This problem is also raised by Chiu (n 20) 213.

poses a threat to consumer trust in the crypto-economy, and potentially their trust in the financial system.[30]

The ability of issuers of unbacked crypto-assets and service providers to evade liability poses a threat to consumer protection. To create legal certainty for all parties, regulation is required to establish rights and obligations for providers and users of unbacked crypto-assets. It is not in alignment with the EU's goals and objectives to leave the legal position of consumers uncertain and dependent on the good will of the service providers in the crypto-economy. With crypto payment's counterpart – being payments in a fiat currency – the legal position of providers and users is regulated under EU legislation.[31] As the market has been unable to secure sufficient consumer protection on its own, it is justified to intervene with regulation to ensure consumer protection. Whether the MiCAR will address these threats will be examined in the following section.

C. MiCAR and the protection of consumers

The Markets in Crypto-Assets Regulation aims to create legal certainty for participants in the crypto ecosystem.[32] Other goals include ensuring financial stability, promoting innovation, and the use of crypto-assets through enhanced consumer and investor protection.[33] Particularly the Regulation's goal of enhancing consumer protection is interesting for the issues treated in this article. The following subsections will examine if and how MiCAR addresses the threats to consumer protection presented above.

1. All cryptocurrencies must be e-money?

When examining MiCAR with a focus on consumer protection and unbacked crypto-assets' function as a means of payment, some provisions and recitals of the Regulation stand out from the rest. Although the recitals hold no legally binding effect on the subjects, they do contribute with context and should function as interpretative contributions when analysing current law.[34]

The primary argument for payments in cryptocurrencies not to be covered by the PSD2 is the missing claim on the issuer for holders of the unbacked crypto-asset.[35] This claim is essential for the E-money Directive's[36] definition of electronic money, or e-money. To rectify this problem, recital 20 first offers a subtle definition of issuers of crypto-assets. Since the MiCAR uses crypto-assets as the overarching term covering all categories or types of crypto-assets, this also includes cryptocurrencies. The recital states:

> Issuers of crypto-assets are entities which have control over the creation of crypto-assets.

The definition can be found in a similar wording in art 3(1)(10) MiCAR which defines 'issuer' as the natural or legal person or other undertaking who issues crypto-assets,

---

[30] ibid 209 also argues the need for a regulatory framework to address needs such as cost and quality in the execution of payments.

[31] Specifically, payments are covered by the PSD2.

[32] MiCAR, recital 6.

[33] MiCAR, recitals 5 and 6.

[34] Case 283/81 *Srl CILFIT and Lanificio di Gavardo SpA v Ministry of Health* ECLI:EU:C:1982:335 para 20.

[35] Chiu (n 20) 209 and Vauplane (n 14) 113.

[36] Directive 2009/110/EC of the European Parliament and of the Council of 16 September 2009 on the taking up, pursuit and prudential supervision of the business of electronic money institutions.

but unlike the recital's wording the legal definition in art 3 does not specify the relationship to the entity being able to control the creation of crypto-assets. The recital therefore holds value in the interpretation of who the issuer of a crypto-asset is.

Another important definition when dealing with payments in unbacked crypto-assets is MiCAR's definition of 'crypto-asset service' which means any of the services and activities listed in art 3(1)(16). The one resembling payments the most is art 3(1)(16)(j) termed 'providing transfer services for crypto-assets on behalf of third parties'. This service is further defined in art 3(1)(26) which defines the service as

> to transfer, on behalf of a natural or legal person, crypto-assets from one distributed ledger address or account to another.

The recitals go further in acknowledging an overlap with payment services, first by supporting the classification of crypto payments under the transfer of crypto-asset service definition in recitals 90 and 93, the former stating:

> some crypto-asset services, in particular custody and administration services, placing of crypto-assets, and transfer services for crypto-assets on behalf of clients, might overlap with payment services as defined in Directive (EU) 2015/2366.

This is expanded upon in recital 93 which provides a lengthy description of the service defined in art 3(1)(26). The recital first identifies the provider of the crypto-asset service as the entity that provides the transfer from one distributed ledger address to another on behalf of a third-party. Continuing, the recital acknowledges that, depending on the precise features of the services provided, these can amount to a payment service as defined in PSD2 and should hence comply with the Directive's rules.

Where these intentions of the legislator clash with reality is in the PSD2's definition of 'funds'. Art 4(1)(25) PSD2 defines 'funds' as banknotes and coins, scriptural money, or electronic money as defined in point (2) of art 2 of Directive 2009/110/EC. This excludes all cryptocurrencies which are not also e-money. The definition of 'funds' is key because the PSD2 refers to this term in its definitions of 'payment systems'[37] and 'payment transactions'[38] which are essential for the PSD2 to be applicable to a transaction covered by the Directive's definition of 'payment service'.[39] The scope created in PSD2, with its narrow definition of funds, effectively excludes all transactions in cryptocurrencies from being covered by the Directive if they cannot also be classified as e-money under the E-money Directive.

To be considered e-money the cryptocurrency must be electronically stored monetary value as represented by a claim on the issuer which is issued on receipt of funds for the purpose of making payment transactions as defined in art 4(1)(5) PSD2. The e-money must be accepted by a natural or legal person other than the e-money issuer.[40] With cryptocurrencies being created on a distributed ledger, it is by nature electronically stored. The monetary value is created through the market's reflection of its value through demand,[41] and as it is possible to pay with cryptocurrencies at an increasing number

[37]PSD2, art 4(1)(7).
[38]PSD2, art 4(1)(5).
[39]PSD2, art 4(1)(3) and Annex 1.
[40]PSD2, art. 2(1)(2).
[41]See Chiu (n 20) 210 for a similar argumentation.

of retailers, other persons than the issuer accepts the token as a payment. The part that has generally not been considered fulfilled is the cryptocurrency representing a claim on the issuer.

MiCAR has already established how to identify the issuer of a cryptocurrency, but does the Regulation also place an obligation upon this entity to provide buyers with a claim on the issuer? Art 49(2) places a duty on issuers to provide holders of e-money tokens with a claim on the issuer. All e-money tokens which does not provide such a claim for the holder on the issuer according to the provision prohibited. This position was also taken in the Regulation's recital 67, which states an intention for all e-money tokens or tokens referencing at least one fiat currency to provide a claim on the issuer. The provision, and the intention, only covers e-money tokens and does therefore not cover unbacked crypto-assets, hence not all cryptocurrencies are e-money. This interpretation of the provision is also supported by the Regulation's definition of e-money tokens which focuses on the token's configuration and not its function. Art 3(1)(7) defines e-money tokens as a type of crypto-asset which purports to maintain a stable value by referencing to the value of one fiat currency. This definition of e-money tokens is potentially in conflict with the definition of e-money in the E-money Directive by focusing on a criterion not present in the Directive and excluding the perhaps most discussed criterion within the cryptocurrency debate – the claim on the issuer.

With this, the MiCAR definition effectively excludes cryptocurrencies not referencing any fiat currency from being covered by the rules of the Regulation, even if the issuer provides holders with a claim against the issuer. This lack of inter-regulatory harmonisation could potentially cause unnecessary harm to holders of unbacked crypto-assets, including consumers.[42] The Regulation leaves the protection of consumers paying in unbacked crypto-assets outside the scope of its regulatory framework by focusing on configuration instead of function.[43] The definition of e-money tokens also squander the potential for cryptocurrencies to become covered by the PSD2's definition of funds as electronic money due to the two definitions being out of sync. Whether the coverage under the crypto-asset transfer service is sufficient to ensure sufficient consumer protection, in place of the full e-money token framework, will be examined further in the next subsection.

2. The dual functionality

The void left for crypto-assets used as a means of payment without being referenced to a fiat currency or other assets, leaves the question whether this group of unbacked crypto-assets is covered by MiCAR? Although an intended function is as a means of payment, or exchange, it cannot be denied that another inherent function is as an investment for the holder. The crypto-assets in question tend to have two possible, co-existing functions – as a means of payment and as a security. This second function also explains how the crypto-asset's value is estimated, including the fluctuations in its value which, as mentioned in section B.2., can be rather volatile.[44]

---

[42] Chiu (n 20) 209 also highlights the need to intervene to solve the volatility problem connected to unbacked crypto-assets.

[43] ibid 208 likewise finds that the functional approach is the most optimal to regulate crypto tokens.

[44] On the lack of stability in value also see European Securities and Markets Authority (n 17) 5.

Returning to the catalyst for the crypto economy – the BitCoin blockchain and bitcoins – the initial purpose was as a decentralised means of payment.[45] Bitcoin has, however, been more popular as an alternative to traditional securities trading, although bitcoin is also accepted as a means of payment at an increasing number of merchants.[46] The two-fold function of bitcoins – and other unbacked crypto-assets falling outside the categorisation created by MiCA – causes problems for consumers paying with cryptocurrencies in good faith, believing their payments to be covered by prudent regulation.[47]

While the function as a security results in the crypto-asset being covered by financial law,[48] such as MIFID2,[49] the crypto-asset's function as a cryptocurrency meant for payments is only covered peripherally by MiCAR. Specifically, MiCAR covers this category and function of the unbacked crypto-asset through the above-presented crypto-asset service termed 'providing transfer services for crypto-assets on behalf of third parties' as defined in art 3(1)(26). The transfer service is regulated in art 82 MiCAR which comprises of a mere two paragraphs. The first paragraph describes mandatory content of the agreement between the service provider and the client, i.e. for the purpose of this article the merchant. The agreement must specify their duties and responsibilities and must at least include the identity of the parties, the modalities of the transfer provided and a description of that service, a description of the security systems used by the crypto-asset service provider, charges applied, and the law applicable to the agreement. As such, the provision does not cover more than basic provisions of a standard contract between service provider and client.

The second paragraph refers to ESMA and EBA who, in close cooperation, have been assigned the task of drafting guidelines regarding procedures and policies for the service providers offering the transfer service. The paragraph specifically mentions to include clients' rights, but this does not refer to the consumers using the service as third parties, it only refers to the merchants being parties to the agreement mandated by paragraph 1. As such, the functionality of the crypto-asset as a payment token is not covered by MiCAR in a way that can ensure the high standards of consumer protection otherwise known within the EU.

Although the payment function is not regulated to a considerable extent, MiCAR does offer what could be termed 'a last resort' under certain circumstances. Art 103(1)(b) provides the ESMA with the option to prohibit or restrict a type of crypto-asset activity or practice. This measure constitutes an extensive intervention in the market for crypto-assets and requires the ESMA to have reasonable grounds that the activity or practice gives rise to significant investor protection concerns, poses a threat to the orderly functioning and integrity of markets in crypto-assets, or to the stability of whole or part of the financial system within at least one Member State. The existing regulatory

[45]As also pointed out by DA Zetzsche and others, 'Liabilities Associated with Distributed Ledgers: A Comparataive Analysis' in Madir (n 3) 193. The idea to denationalise money was most prominently disseminated by FA von Hayek, *Denationalisation of Money* (The Institute of Economic Affairs 1976).

[46]The number of merchants accepting crypto payments is expected to be rising, see Deloitte (n 3) and the demand among consumers is increasing as well according to Cabuk and Silenzi (n 3).

[47]Financial Conduct Authority (n 8) found that 5% of consumers using crypto believed they had some form of protection and 12% believed their cryptocurrency investments had financial protection.

[48]For more on the categorisation and applicable law to security tokens see L Damkjær Christensen, 'Initial Coin Offerings – Are Tokens Transferable Securities?' (2022) Nordisk Tidsskrift for Selskabsret (Nordic Journal for Company Law) 44.

[49]Directive 2014/65/EU of the European Parliament and of the Council of 15 May 2014 on markets in financial instruments.

requirements must also be found insufficient to address these risks and the improvement of supervision and enforcement must also be insufficient. Furthermore, the restriction or prohibition must be proportionate taking into account the nature of the risks, the level of sophistication of investors or market participants concerned, and the likely effect of the action on investors and market participants who may hold, use, or benefit from the crypto-asset or service. As crypto-assets are generally considered cross-border, the ESMA must also have consulted competent authorities in Member States which may be significantly affected by the restriction or prohibition. Finally, the restriction or prohibition must not have a discriminatory effect on services or activities provided from another Member State.[50] When a crypto-asset activity or practice poses such threats will, according to art 103(8), be specified by the Commission in delegated acts. Although this ensures greater harmonisation across Member States, it also holds the potential to delay such intervention unnecessarily having to wait for the Commission's drafting of the acts.

With MiCAR essentially only covering payments in cryptocurrencies through its art 82, which provides little comfort for consumers, the problem of systemic risks created through different regulation of the same function continues to exist along with the unbacked crypto-asset's volatility and the lack of liability.

The dual functionality of crypto-assets which are both used as an investment, being covered by existing financial law, and as a means of payment, would seem not to have been addressed by MiCAR. While MiCAR does not intend to provide further or different regulation for the security function of the crypto-asset, market participants should have been provided with legal certainty regarding the payment function of the same unbacked crypto-asset. The choice not to address this issue in MiCAR can lead to different conclusions. One option is that the use of, for example, bitcoin but also other unbacked crypto-assets, as a payment for goods does in fact not involve a payment but instead an exchange of a security token for a good. Where this leaves consumers, and their protection, is rather unclear. The second option does not provide much comfort for consumers either as it would leave it to the crypto market to set the conditions for payments in cryptocurrencies. Whether a consumer then holds a right of recourse, rectification, or protection against fraud is left for the transfer service provider and merchant to decide.

3. Liability and accountability

A well-known feature of distributed ledger technology is its immutability and finality. Once a transaction has been initiated it cannot be reversed.[51] While this characteristic holds many advantages for seasoned actors on the crypto-asset market, it constitutes a problem when it comes to wrongful payments or crypto-fraud.[52] And when considering consumers using unbacked crypto-assets as a means of payment, the problem becomes grave. Where the PSD2 provides an extensive ruleset to regulate situations of wrongful execution or payments fraud, the MiCAR does not contain any such provisions related to the provision of the transfer of crypto-assets service.

The Regulation's art 82 only regulates the minimum requirements to the contract between the transfer service provider and the client – the merchant. The accountability

[50] MiCAR, art 103(2),(3), (4), and (5).
[51] Also see Baker and Werbach (n 3) 127 and Zetzsche and others (n 45) 187.
[52] This problem is also raised by Chiu (n 20) 213.

can be prescribed to the contract's description of the security systems used by the crypto-asset service provider, but whether these security measures include the consumer using the service through the merchant is uncertain. This leaves the question of the consumer's legal position in case of wrongful execution and fraudulent transactions open for the market to govern. Without incentives for market actors to provide proper consumer protection, it is unlikely that consumers will have any protection when paying with unbacked crypto-assets.

Despite the EU legislator aiming to ensure consumer protection in the crypto-economy, the MiCAR falls short on this aspect when it comes to payments in unbacked crypto-assets.

D. What cards does the EU policymaker hold?

The evaluation of MiCAR's management of the threats to consumer protection described in section B indicates a missed opportunity to address these issues. This perception is also supported by the ESMA in the 2022 Report on Trends, Risks and Vulnerabilities Risk Analysis on crypto-assets and their risks for financial stability.[53] The report highlights risks of a potential wide-spread adoption of unregulated assets and related risks for the purpose of transactions using crypto-assets as a means of payment and settlement.[54] The report goes further to indicate the risks related to consumer exposure if more large retailers or leading tech companies implement crypto-asset-based payments, although the scale of this remains limited currently.[55]

Leaving the crypto-economy to develop consumer protection mechanisms has so far proved unfruitful. As such, it cannot be expected that the market will provide these mechanisms which the legislator desire and expect to be present in a market which includes consumers.[56] Although some have argued that responsible innovation in the crypto-economy is possible,[57] the MiCAR is evidence that the EU legislator has deemed regulatory intervention necessary to secure the stability and functioning of the internal market after crypto-assets' advent.[58] This section will evaluate on the MiCAR's ability to address the threats identified and discuss the possible options for the EU legislator to improve consumer protection in relation to payments in unbacked crypto-assets.

1. Amending MiCAR

The first solution would be to amend the MiCAR expanding art 82 to include measures to protect consumers initiating transactions covered by an agreement between a crypto-asset service provider and a merchant. This would address direct issues related to the consumer position in these transactions and could provide rights and obligations on all

[53]European Securities and Markets Authority (n 17).

[54]ibid 12.

[55]ibid.

[56]Chiu (n 20) 215 also advocates for a strong regulatory framework to create optimal circumstances for the payment function of unbacked crypto-assets.

[57]See J Durham, 'Regulatory Sandboxes Enable Pragmatic Blockchain Regulation' (2023) 18 Washington Journal of Law, Technology & Arts 29, 46 coming to the conclusion that regulatory intervention is necessary in most aspects of the crypto-economy.

[58]This conclusion is also supported by Chiu (n 20) 210 and J Lee, 'Law and Regulation for a Crypto-market – Perpetuation or Innovation?' in Chiu and Deipenbrock (n 4) 370.

parties to protect the weakest party – the consumer. As such, consumers would experience greater legal certainty when paying in unbacked crypto-assets.

Although an amendment of MiCAR could provide necessary consumer protection, particularly in relation to liability and execution of transactions, it would not address other pressing issues. Using unbacked crypto-assets as a means of payment and covering the transactions under a new regulatory framework does not address the potential systemic risks caused by applying different regulations to the same function. Having MiCAR cover payments in crypto-assets, instead of expanding the scope of PSD2, would create two parallel regulatory frameworks regulating the same function but discriminating based on underlying technology. To ensure similar consumer protection as provided under the PSD2 would also require extensive additions to the MiCAR, a Regulation the EU co-legislators have not come to an agreement on easily.

Another issue, which an amendment to the MiCAR would not solve, is the volatility problem inherent to unbacked crypto-assets. Although by nature these crypto-assets are unsuited as a means of payment due to their volatile value, lack of price transparency, and low liquidity,[59] the bitcoin was created with this specific purpose in mind. With options to pay for goods in crypto-assets increasing,[60] it is necessary for regulators to find a solution to address the volatility problem of unbacked crypto-assets. A possible solution could be for regulators to require payments in crypto-assets to only be made using e-money tokens, stablecoins, or CBDCs, but is it possible to enforce such a requirement this late in the crypto-game?

2. *The revision of the PSD2*

As already established, crypto-assets which are not e-money tokens are not covered by the scope of the PSD2. Fortunately, the Directive is currently under revision by the European Commission.[61] With the newly adopted Transfer of funds Regulation[62] to include crypto-assets in its scope, there is hope that the EU legislator will follow suit with a similar update on the 'funds' definition in the PSD2, expanding the scope to also cover unbacked crypto-assets when used for payments.

Expanding the scope of the PSD2 to include payments in crypto-assets would provide considerable comfort for consumers – improving consumer protection – and could aid the goal of innovation by making payments in crypto-assets safer from a legal point of view.[63] Covering crypto-asset payments under the PSD2 does not solve the volatility problem,[64] but it does address the problem related to systemic risks rising from applying different legislation to the same function. Revising the PSD2 to also cover payments in unbacked crypto-assets would level the playing-field on the payments market and

[59]See also Hermans and others (n 20) section 3.

[60]See Cabuk and Silenzi (n 3) and Deloitte (n 3).

[61]European Commission, 'Consultation Document: Targeted Consultation on the Review of the Revised Payment Services Directive (PSD2)' (2022).

[62]Regulation (EU) 2023/1113 of the European Parliament and of the Council of 31 May 2023 on information accompanying transfers of funds and certain crypto-assets.

[63]Chiu (n 20) 210 also promotes the use of regulation to mitigate the hazards for users of unbacked crypto-assets for payment purposes.

[64]ibid 209 offers two rather restrictive solutions to the volatility problem but neither entails cryptocurrencies continuing in the currently known form.

provide for fairer competition between the more traditional payments, third-party payments, and crypto-asset payments.

The issues related to accountability and liability would also be addressed through the thorough liability regime of the PSD2, which ensures sufficient security for consumers opting to pay in unbacked crypto-assets. Although increased consumer protection is a well-known objective for the EU, the improved safety of consumers would come at the cost of placing more risk and costs on providers of payments in crypto-assets. By making the provider of the payment service liable for fraud or wrongfully executed transfers, as covered by the PSD2's arts 71–74, and the security provisions in the Directive's chapter 5, the legislator moves the risks related to paying with crypto-assets from the consumer to the service provider, potentially decreasing their incentives to offer the service. Though, this is already the working circumstances for payment service providers covered under the PSD2 and would hence contribute to levelling the playing-field. Finally, this trade-off – improving consumer protection at the cost of risking a smaller decrease in innovation – is a small price to pay for securing a payments market in regulatory balance.

3. Restricting unbacked crypto-assets

The last option to be considered here is to restrict, or outright ban, the use of unbacked crypto-assets as a means of payment. In favour of such a restriction are the objectives of ensuring extensive consumer protection, fair competition, and protecting financial stability across the EU. The threats which this use of unbacked crypto-assets pose to the functioning of the financial system cannot be counterbalanced by the objective to advance financial innovation. Albeit innovation can contribute to growth and general improvements in society, it cannot be assumed regardless that letting innovation roam freely is always the best solution.

Where adopting restrictions or a ban on the use of unbacked crypto-assets for payments is a rather simple process for the European Parliament, the practicalities of implementing and enforcing such restrictions are much difficult, if not impossible. The crypto-economy exists in the online realm and is based on decentralised ledger technology, essentially creating their own community.[65] The efforts to regulate the crypto-economy is difficult as it is, but creating a ban on specific functions within the EU will only push such activities outside of the EU potentially resulting in even less safety for consumers.

Furthermore, restricting the use of unbacked crypto-assets would be in conflict with the current regulatory policy adopted by the EU. This approach would also with some certainty work against MiCAR's goal of increasing the adoption of crypto-assets in the Union.[66] Imposing restrictions that essentially ban a specific activity would be contrary to the approach adopted by the EU, where a wait-and-see approach has been most widely used. Considering the other options available, it is easy to conclude that restricting or banning payments in unbacked crypto-assets is not a viable, if even possible, solution and cannot be recommended to the EU legislator.

[65] In the online realm, it could also be discussed who holds jurisdiction, but such discussions are extensive and beyond the subject of this article.

[66] Proposal for MiCA Regulation, recitals 4 and 5.

E. Conclusion

The examination of the MiCA Regulation establishes that a legal vacuum of uncertainty for consumers remain in the crypto economy. The use of unbacked crypto-assets, or cryptocurrencies, as a means of payment is briefly regulated in MiCAR as the transfer of crypto-assets service in the Regulation's art 82. Unfortunately, the provision only regulates the minimum requirements for the contract between the service provider and the client – the merchant. This leaves the threats of volatility, potential systemic risks, and the lack of accountability and liability for the market to manage. As such, the MiCAR does not address the issues surrounding payments in unbacked crypto-assets and leaves the consumer protection endangered.

With the threats to consumer protection still unmanaged, possible solutions to address these were considered. Considering the EU legislator's objectives – aiming to promote innovation and the application of cryptographic technology and to protect consumers from undue harm – the solution which would balance the threats and objectives best is the revision of the PSD2. By including payments in unbacked crypto-assets, or cryptocurrencies, to the scope of the PSD2 through an expansion of the 'funds' definition in the Directive's art 4 (1)(25), most of the threats to consumer protection would be addressed. The described potential systemic risks would be avoided as all payment service providers would be covered under the same regulatory framework, and consumers would be safe when using crypto payment transactions in regard to accountability and liability. The last threat of unbacked crypto-assets' volatility, inherently a characteristic of the asset, would seem near impossible for legislation to solve without imposing extensive restrictions to the nature of the asset.

While MiCAR has generally made intermediaries a necessity in the crypto economy, the need for regulation of such intermediaries in crypto payments has not been addressed by the regulation. Regulating the payment function of unbacked crypto-assets does not have to infer a status as 'money' or 'legal tender' on the national level, but regulating the function is a necessity because of the market's demand of this function. Choosing to leave payments in unbacked crypto-assets out of scope in EU regulation is to leave consumers' legal status to chance, something that was otherwise considered unnatural in EU law.

Acknowledgements

I would like to express my gratitude to the conference organisers, the participants, and fellow presenters at the Institute for Advanced Legal Studies' 2022 conference on Cryptocurrencies, Smart Contracts, and Alternative Payments for your interesting thoughts and inputs on an early draft of this article. I am also grateful to the anonymous reviewers who provided me with useful comments. Any errors or omissions are solely my responsibility.

Disclosure statement

No potential conflict of interest was reported by the author(s).

ORCID

Louise Damkjær Christensen http://orcid.org/0000-0002-7384-6977

Smart contracts: to regulate or not? Global perspectives

Pınar Çağlayan Aksoy

ABSTRACT

Smart contracts continue to formulate the backbone of blockchain transactions. After the foundation of the Ethereum protocol, the Initial Coin Offerings, Security Token Offerings, and Non-Fungible Tokens have all relied on smart contracts, with enormous market volume. The broad scope of smart contracts' (potential) application is undisputed, yet many countries have been silent on the regulation of smart contracts. These same countries, however, have already set some standards regarding crypto assets and crypto asset service providers. We can include Switzerland and the European Union, that has already prepared a draft Regulation for Markets in Crypto Assets, in this first group. Some jurisdictions, such as the UK and the US, have already concluded that common law principles suffice to tackle with smart contracts. The third group, including Italy, has defined smart contracts but has no comprehensive regulatory framework. There is a final group of countries that have chosen not to regulate any aspects of the distributed ledger technology (yet). It is without a doubt that the use of smart contracts will cause problems regarding formation, contract performance, applicable law, jurisdiction, protection of consumers, and personal data.

A. Introduction

Smart contracts are having their renaissance with the wide adoption of distributed ledger technology. The term 'smart contract' was coined by Nick Szabo at the beginning of the 1990s. Back then, Szabo was referring to a computerised transaction protocol that executes the terms of a contract.[1] Smart contracts were deemed to have the potential to go beyond the simple vending machine in proposing to embed contracts in all sorts of property that is valuable and controlled by digital means.[2] Although some financial companies have been implementing this idea without specifically referring to the phrase 'smart contract', the technological infrastructure was not developed enough to realise Szabo's ideals. After the launch of Ethereum protocol, Szabo stated in 2016 that 'Blockchain technology appears very much to be the jet fuel necessary for smart contracts to

[1] N Szabo, 'Smart Contracts' (1994) <https://www.fon.hum.uva.nl/rob/Courses/InformationInSpeech/CDROM/Literature/LOTwinterschool2006/szabo.best.vwh.net/smart.contracts.html> accessed 25 January 2023.

[2] Ni Szabo, Smart Contracts: Building Blocks for Digital Markets (1996) <https://www.fon.hum.uva.nl/rob/Courses/InformationInSpeech/CDROM/Literature/LOTwinterschool2006/szabo.best.vwh.net/smart_contracts_2.html> accessed 25 January 2023.

become commonplace in business transactions and beyond'.[3] This was a kick-off for many legal considerations with regard to smart contracts.

Smart contracts are computer programmes that run on the blockchain, based on a pre-defined conditional logic (*if this ... then that*). Parties write a contract in coding language (or have it designed by a professional) and publish it on a blockchain which is maintained by developers and miners. They eliminate the need for central intermediaries between parties, hence they lower transaction costs.[4] Since smart contracts are based on automation and self-enforcement,[5] they – in a sense – guarantee the performance of the agreed outcome. This attribute reduces the enforcement costs.[6] Smart contracts act as the foundational software layer for coding utility, applications (e.g. decentralised applications: 'Dapps')[7] and programmable functions into the blockchain.[8]

The enforceability of smart contracts under private law is an issue of debate.[9] The content, legal status, auditability, execution, and reliability of smart contracts are not regulated and unclear in many jurisdictions. According to an OECD report, 'until it is clarified whether contract law applies to smart contracts, enforceability and financial protection issues will persist'.[10] This also leads to the difficulty of determining the parameters for the protection of consumers and privacy. Since there are multiple jurisdictions involved in transactions regarding smart contracts, the resolution of these problems is even more challenging.[11]

The regulation of smart contracts has been considered from various perspectives by many authors with a single point of focus: consumer protection, contractual remedies, data protection, etc. Smart contracts do not affect only a single area of law and in fact regulating only one these areas would not be enough to protect the market, consumers

[3]Chamber of Digital Commerce, 'Smart Contracts: 12 Use Cases for Business & Beyond: A Technology, Legal & Regulatory Introduction – Foreword by Nick Szabo' (2016) <https://d3h0qzni6h08fz.cloudfront.net/Smart-Contracts-12-Use-Cases-for-Business-and-Beyond_Chamber-of-Digital-Commerce.pdf> accessed 25 January 2023, 3.

[4]A Ferreira, 'Regulating smart contracts: Legal revolution or simply evolution' (2021) 45 Telecommunications Policy 1, 4.

[5]M Durovic and F Lech, 'The Enforceability of Smart Contracts' (2019) 5 Italian Law Journal, 493, 498; S Green and A Sanitt, 'Smart Contracts' in PS Davies and M Raczynska (eds), *The Contents of Commercial Contracts: Terms Affecting Freedoms* (Hart 2020) 191.

[6]M Kaulartz, 'Herausforderungen bei der Gestaltung von Smart Contracts' (2016) 4 Zeitschrift zum Innovations- und Technikrecht 201, 203; JM Sklaroff, 'Smart Contracts and the Cost of Inflexibility' (2018) 9 Prize Winning Papers 263, 275; K Werbach and N Cornell, 'Contracts *Ex Machina*' (2017) 67 Duke Law Journal 313, 335; O Borgogno, 'Smart Contracts as the (new) Power of the Powerless? The Stakes for Consumers' (2019) 26 (6) European Review of Private Law 885, 888; K Kasprzyk, 'The Concept of Smart Contracts from the Legal Perspective' (2018) 34 Review of Comparative Law 101, 104.

[7]DeFi allows non-sophisticated parties to easily participate in otherwise inaccessible financial transactions using decentralised applications. Dapps are pieces of software stored on the blockchain and run by smart contracts. DApps can be used to lend money, pool money to invest in assets, or get insurance.

[8]Global X Research Team [2022] <https://www.globalxetfs.com/exploring-the-disruptive-potential-of-smart-contracts/> accessed 25 January 2023.

[9]M Durovic and F Lech: 'The Enforceability of Smart Contracts' (2019) 5(2) Italian Law Journal 493–512; M Raskin 'The Law and Legality of Smart Contracts' (2017) 301(1) Georgetown Law Technology Review 305–41; Clifford Chance and European Bank for Reconstruction and Development, Smart Contracts: Legal Framework and Proposed Guidelines For Lawmakers, p. 11.

[10]'The legal status of smart contracts still remains to be defined' OECD, The Tokenisation of Assets and Potential Implications for Financial Markets (2020) OECD Blockchain Policy Series at 20, www.oecd.org/finance/The-Tokenisation-of-Assets-and-PotentialImplications-for-Financial-Markets.htm.

[11]OECD, 'Regulatory Approaches to the Tokenisation of Assets' (2021) <www.oecd.org/finance/Regulatory-Approaches-to-the-Tokenisation-of-Assets.htm> accessed 25 January 2023, 32. According to Sir Geoffrey Vos the use of smart contracts would increase if there is legal clarity about the legal enforceability of contractual provisions expressed in code, about how such provisions will be interpreted, and about what parties can do when things go wrong with the code. G Vos, 'End-to-End Smart Legal Contracts: Moving from Aspiration to Reality' in J Allen and P Hunn (eds), *Smart Legal Contracts: Computable Law in Theory and Practice* (Oxford Academic, 23 June 2022) 57.

and investors. This paper therefore endorses a more holistic approach in the sense that it offers a comparative framework to guide the regulators and policy makers on the crucial legal issues that need to be considered if the regulatory path is chosen. This article unfolds as follows: first, we explain the true potential of smart contracts and the areas in which they are commonly used. Then we focus on the legal problems that arise from smart contracts and underline the fact that smart contracts are not without hassle. Third we elaborate on the possible regulatory considerations when it comes to smart contracts. We specifically focus on the countries and regulatory bodies that endorse the wait and see approach, opt for regulation, or decide not to regulate smart contracts. Finally, we discuss the main issues that needs to be considered by the law makers if regulation is chosen as the path to follow.

B. The true potential of smart contracts

According to some, the magic that blockchain networks have to offer, is largely materialised using smart contracts.[12] Let's go back in time: It all started with a potential to disrupt the traditional financial services industry. This was the main idea behind Bitcoin.[13] Then came smart contracts, the famous well-known applications on blockchain. They were seen as the next step toward 'making finance even more software-centric'.[14] The decentralised applications ('Dapps') hosted on smart contract blockchains have been assuming the potential to disrupt lending and payments, insurance, brokerage, investments, and foreign exchange services.[15] But there is no doubt that smart contracts are so much more than finance today.[16]

Although they are seen in the infancy phase, they still hold a significant place in the blockchain ecosystem. Smart contracts are used in blockchain platforms to digitally define, create, and represent different assets. Smart contracts transfer and manage crypto-assets (tokens).[17] They enable tokenisation of goods, services, or rights.[18] Real estate, digital content, art, ownership rights can all be tokenised as units of account on or off-chain.[19] Smart contracts also define rights and obligations and make sure that these are implemented through the life cycle of a digital asset. Generally, the tokenisation process is carried out by an Initial Coin Offering (ICO). The tokens offered in the ICO are

[12]GC Polemidiotis, 'Smart Contracts and the New Reality' [2022] <https://www.llpolawfirm.com/2022/02/21/smart-contracts-and-the-new-reality/> accessed 25 January 2023.

[13]S Nakamoto, 'Bitcoin: A Peer-to-Peer Electronic Cash System' <https://bitcoin.org/bitcoin.pdf> accessed 25 January 2023.

[14]Global X Research Team [2022] <https://www.globalxetfs.com/exploring-the-disruptive-potential-of-smart-contracts/> accessed 25 January 2023.

[15]Today there are approximately 256,730 smart contracts tracked across all protocols. The total number of dapps tracked across all protocols is 13,275. When the total number of unique active wallets interacting with the smart contracts per category in the specified period is observed, games have the highest number followed by DeFi. The world's Dapp store: Discover, track & trade everything DeFi, NFT and gaming <https://dappradar.com/industry-overview> accessed 25 January 2023.

[16]Global X ETFs [2022] <https://www.nasdaq.com/articles/an-investors-guide-to-smart-contract-blockchains> accessed 25 January 2023.

[17]J Cieplak and S Leefatt, 'Smart Contracts: A Smart Way to Automate Performance' (2017) 1 Georgia L & Tech Rev 417.

[18]R Prabucki and others, 'Algorithmisation and Tokenisation of Law' in D Szostek and M Załucki (eds), *Legal Tech Information technology tools in the administration of justice* (Nomos 2021) 44.

[19]Depending on the standard used in the smart contract protocol, a token can be fungible or non-fungible. See P Çağlayan Aksoy and Z Özkan Üner, 'NFTs and copyright: challenges and opportunities' (2021) 16(10) Journal of Intellectual Property Law & Practice 1115.

distributed via smart contracts.[20] Hence, smart contracts are the backbone of tokenisation.[21]

In the realm of securities, smart contracts can automate compliance with laws and regulations. Smart contracts are used by some exchanges to automate securities transactions and be involved in various processes during the securities trading cycle. Shares and bonds can be encoded into a smart contract to represent the tokenised interest.[22] The use of smart contracts have the potential reduce the cost of issuing and administering securities.[23] Well-designed smart contracts can reduce the need for intermediaries and reduce counterparty and operational risks[24] by eliminating risk points in a transaction.

Smart contracts can be used to automate purchasing process and payment automation. In the field of intellectual property law, smart contracts can facilitate and automate income for authors. They can be used for IP rights management. Authors can publish works on the blockchain and then 'use smart contracts to automate the control of who has access to their works and under which conditions' to obtain remuneration.[25]

Smart contracts can be used in the insurance industry to create products that instantly and automatically make payments when conditions predefined in the smart contract code occurs. Therefore, the need for a lengthy and costly claim validation process is eliminated.[26]

Smart contracts can also be used to create business entities and control their governance structure. These new entities called DAOs (decentralised autonomous organisations) are defined by the UK Law Commission as 'a novel type of technology-mediated social structure or organisation of participants'.[27] The organisational structure is formulated and managed by smart contracts. The governance rules and activities (participation, realisation of financial transactions, decision-making, voting, etc.) of the DAO are coded with smart contracts. It is also the smart contract that automates the enforcement of these rules deterministically.[28] A DAO can carry out its business without a physical presence because it is managed in a decentralised manner by a network of smart contracts deployed to a blockchain system. This results in the reduction of human oversight compared to a traditional, centrally managed organisation. The participants of a DAO interact with each other through blockchain-based software protocols and smart contracts.[29] There is a great interest on DAOs, and many initiatives exist all around the globe. It is

---

[20]Prabucki and others (n 18) 44.

[21]Among the challenges before the wide adoption of asset tokenisation lies the legal status of smart contracts. Technology-related challenges, governance risk arising especially from AML/CFT requirements, digital identity and data protection and privacy. OECD (n 10) 7.

[22]Goldman Sachs, 'Digitizing Bonds on the Blockchain' (2021) <https://www.goldmansachs.com/insights/pages/from_briefings_10-june-2021.html> accessed 25 January 2023.

[23]'Automation introduced in the issuance, distribution, management of securities but also around securities servicing and corporate actions may reduce costs throughout the securities transaction lifetime, benefiting issuers and investors alike' OECD (n 10) 16.

[24]EU Blockchain Observatory and Forum, 'Smart Contracts 2022' at 6, <https://www.eublockchainforum.eu/sites/default/files/reports/SmartContractsReport_Final.pdf> accessed 25 January 2023.

[25]B Bodó, D Gervais and JP Quintais, 'Blockchain and Smart Contracts: The Missing Link in Copyright Licensing?' (2018) 26 (4) International Journal of Law and Information Technology 333.

[26]European Insurance and Occupational Pensions Authority (EIOPA), 'Discussion Paper on Blockchain and Smart Contracts in Insurance' (2021) <https://www.eiopa.europa.eu/sites/default/files/publications/consultations/eiopa-discussion-paper-on-blockchain-29-04-2021.pdf≥ accessed 25 January 2023.

[27]UK Law Commission, 'Decentralised autonomous organisations (DAOs) Call for evidence' (2022) 1.

[28]Decentralised Autonomous Organisations, <https://ethereum.org/en/dao/≥ accessed 25 January 2023.

[29]UK Law Commission (n 27).

possible to create value through DAOs. The legal status and liability of DAOs is an urging topic in private law. Some jurisdictions, for instance some states in the USA have already enacted specific legislation regarding DAOs by recognising them as an LLC. There also some efforts in the international level for reaching a unified legal approach toward DAOs.[30] In June 2023, a district court in the US has declared that the DAO in question is a person under the US Commodity Exchange Act. This has created a precedent that DAOs are legal entities that can be held liable for their actions.[31]

Smart contracts are also used in trade finance and supply chain management. Smart contracts can be set up as an escrow account that monitors the exchange between parties. It can track the location of the goods and when ownership is transferred it can trigger payments. Smart contracts can automatically distinguish when each step of the supply chain is carried out without risk of fraud or need for manual recording. Smart contracts can, speed up delivery, provide transparency and reduce the possibility of theft.[32]

Smart contracts have important advantages for identity management as well: Verifiable credentials can allow 'sharing medical data directly from the issuer to the holder without the need to store the data. Smart contracts can be leveraged to orchestrate this process. Additionally, smart contracts can be used to anonymise data'.[33]

We have demonstrated that smart contracts have many current and potential use cases and they are the heart and soul of blockchain technology. Almost every blockchain transaction has a potential to end up with a legal question surrounding smart contracts. However, laying down legal rules governing blockchain and blockchain applications is not an easy task. Many countries have already enacted legislation to mitigate concerns over security, consumer protection and financial crime aspects of blockchain.[34] According to a report prepared by the Swiss Federal Council in 2018, the reason why the focus is on the financial sector is that regulatory questions were particularly critical considering developments in cryptocurrencies and initial coin offerings (ICOs).[35] There have been many risks and scandals tied to the issuance, offering and exchange of crypto assets and crypto asset service providers which required more immediate regulatory response. Stronger financial regulations were seen as the first step for addressing many concerns about the crypto ecosystem.

Although smart contracts play an important role in the value chain within the blockchain ecosystem and in many different sectors, it is not easy to reach a uniform approach regarding the enforceability, security, and reliability of smart contracts. For instance, the insurance industry is seen as a well-suited candidate for the adoption of smart contracts since it relies on digitally verifiable events.[36] Although many institutions are interested in

---

[30]See COALA Model Law for Decentralised Autonomous Organisations (2021), https://coala.global/wp-content/uploads/2021/06/DAOModel-Law.pdf accessed 4 May 2023.

[31]'Statement of CFTC Division of Enforcement Director Ian McGinley on the Ooki DAO Litigation Victory' (*CTFC*, 9 June 2023) https://www.cftc.gov/PressRoom/PressReleases/8715-23, accessed 13 June 2023.

[32]DHK Trend Research, 'Blockchain in Logistics – Perspectives on the Upcoming Impact of Blockchain Technology and Use Cases for the Logistics Industry' (2018) 12–18 www.logistics.dhl/content/dam/dhl/global/core/documents/pdf/glo-core-blockchain-trend-report.pdf accessed 25 January 2023.

[33]EU Blockchain Observatory and Forum (n 24) at 25–26.

[34]Chamber of Digital Commerce (n 3).

[35]Swiss Federal Council Report, 'Legal framework for distributed ledger technology and blockchain in Switzerland: An overview with a focus on the financial sector' (14 December 2018) 11 https://www.newsd.admin.ch/newsd/message/attachments/55153.pdf> accessed 25 January 2023.

[36]In the insurance sector, smart contracts can increase efficiency in underwriting, pricing and claims processing, reduce the risk of errors and disputes, streamline information exchange and payments between insurers and reinsurers,

using blockchain technology for insurance, since smart contracts are still unregulated, many aspects remain unclear for the actors.[37] The self-executing and immutable nature of smart contracts could cause damage against an insured party with inappropriate claim denials. Where there is legal uncertainty about the potential implications for the insurance market, there is a barrier to the use of smart contracts in the sector. The lack of an established framework leads to divergent regulatory and supervisory practices in insurance and different level of consumer protection across the EU.[38]

The time has come to discuss if smart contracts should also be regulated like crypto assets and crypto asset service providers. It is important to focus on the regulation of smart contracts sooner than later.[39] There are several reasons for this. First, smart contracts have a convergence with AI systems, and this is becoming more evident every day AI becomes mainstream.[40] Smart contracts have important features that make them significant for the future of AI and 5G automation.[41] Moreover, smart contracts are suited to be the key technology for the emergence of AI-enhanced super-intelligent control of economic activity. AI-enhanced smart contracts can increase efficiency, improve accuracy, reduce costs and enhance the security of digital transactions.[42] These improvements will lead to higher adoption of smart contracts. In addition to the AI integration, the rising transaction volumes of NFTs and DAOs in the last few years, which are in a way 'complex smart contracts' or 'chains of smart contracts' make it more crucial that smart contracts are dealt with from a legal perspective. Finally, since smart contracts operate on a transnational basis, compatibility, standardisation and interoperability should be ensured promptly. The parties involved in a smart contract transaction should be able to seek legal redress irrespective of the country of origin.

According to CoinDesk Indices, the smart contract platform[43] sector is the second largest sector in digital asset classification standards, right after currency.[44] Although smart contracts have the potential to revolutionise many industries, it is of common understanding that they have not reached their full potential. In the report titled 'Insights, Inputs, and Recommendations to EU Blockchain Regulatory Efforts', start-ups were asked

automate a large part of the claims-handling process, and facilitate the client onboarding process. A Prebble, 'Blockchain and Smart Contracts in Insurance, The advantages of a coordinated approach' (9 July 2021) https://www.cliffordchance.com/insights/resources/blogs/talking-tech/en/articles/2021/07/blockchain-and-smart-contracts-in-insurance.html accessed 5 May 2023.

[37]'How to Make a Smart Contract Work for the Insurance Industry' (18 January 2022), <https://intellias.com/how-to-make-a-smart-contract-work-for-the-insurance-industry/#:~:text=With%20smart%20contracts%2C%20insurers%20will,and%20smart%20contracts%20in%20particular> accessed 25 January 2023.

[38]EIOPA (n 26) 29.

[39]In the same stance see, J Arcari, 'Note, Decoding Smart Contracts: Technology, Legitimacy, and Legislative Uniformity' (2019) 24 Fordham J. Corp. & Fin. L. 363, 395.

[40]A Borselli, 'Smart Contracts in Insurance: A Law and Futurology Perspective' in P Marano and K Noussia (eds) *InsurTech: A Legal and Regulatory View. AIDA Europe Research Series on Insurance Law and Regulation* (Springer 2020) 112: 'It is nevertheless possible to predict a world where smart contracts, combined with future developments in artificial intelligence and machine learning, might challenge traditional views and change contracting practices, automating the entire contractual relationship of the parties.'

[41]W Lehr, 'Smart Contracts: Myths and Implications for Economics and Financial Regulation', 31st European Conference of the International Telecommunications Society (ITS): 'Reining in Digital Platforms? Challenging monopolies, promoting competition, and developing regulatory regimes', Gothenburg, Sweden, 20th–21st June 2022, International Telecommunications Society (ITS), Calgary, 36.

[42]Solidity Academy, Combining Smart Contracts with Artificial Intelligence in Solidity (30 April 2023) https://medium.com/coinmonks/combining-smart-contracts-with-artificial-intelligence-in-solidity-c88fa25d059> accessed 5 May 2023.

[43]The most widely used platforms to develop and execute smart contracts can be listed as, Ethereum, Hyperledger, Polkadot, Solana, Cosmos and Stellar. EU Blockchain Observatory and Forum (n 24) at 8.

[44]CoinDesk Indices (13 May 2022). Market capitalisation data is based on 30 April 2022.

about their priorities ranking. They rated the regulation of smart contracts as the main priority for more extensive blockchain adoption.[45] Moreover, according to respondent start-ups, the most significant barrier to the use of smart contracts was the vague legal framework.

In the next part, we draw attention to the fact that not only regulation is timely, but it is also necessary since smart contracts can and do cause legal problems and uncertainty.

C. Smart contracts are not without challenges

When smart contracts became mainstream, many people started discussing the idea of 'code is law'.[46] Accordingly, whatever the parties decided and reflected in code would be enforced by the smart contract and the parties must endorse the outcome no matter what. Since smart contracts are stored and automatically executed with the help of blockchain technology, contract law and in fact the entire legal system becomes obsolete. This means that smart contracts are governed only by code and not by state laws. According to an author, 'smart contracts do not need a legal system for their existence: they may operate without any overarching legal framework. De facto, they represent a technological alternative to the whole legal system'.[47]

However, after almost 10 years of discussing smart contracts, we have had enough experience with them to conclude that they are not without trouble. And when these problems occur, legal rules will be applied since smart contracts do not exist in a legal vacuum.[48]

There are many potential problems surrounding the formation, performance, and execution of smart contracts which may introduce significant challenges for the participants in the smart contract ecosystem. And there are even more reasons why people and entities interacting with smart contracts will need to resort to legal rules:

First, smart contracts are mostly coded by humans. Codes are prone to coding errors and bugs.[49] These errors can be unintentional or intentional. For instance, the coder can intentionally include flaws in code to enable funds being removed from a wallet. The coder can also create a contract that operates as a pyramid scheme, with a bug that allows funds to be taken outside of the original parameters.[50] The smart contract may execute its terms in a way that does not comply with the will of the parties, or it may make an incorrect assessment as to whether the terms are fulfilled or not.[51]

---

[45]'Report on Insights, Inputs and Recommendations to EU Blockchain Regulatory Efforts' (2022) <https://b-hub.eu/wp-content/uploads/2022/03/B-HUB_Report-on-insightsinputsrecommendations-to-EU-regulatory-efforts.pdf> accessed 25 January 2023.

[46]L Lessig, *Code and Other Laws of Cyberspace* (Basic Books 1999).

[47]A Savalyev, 'Contract Law 2.0: 'Smart' contracts as the beginning of the end of classic contract law' (2017) 26 Information & Communication Technology Law 116, 132.

[48]C Lim, TJ Saw and C Sargeant, Smart Contracts: Bridging the Gap Between Expectation and Reality (11 July 2016) https://blogs.law.ox.ac.uk/business-law-blog/blog/2016/07/smart-contracts-bridging-gap-between-expectation-and-reality accessed 25 May 2023.

[49]C Poncibò and L DiMatteo, 'Smart Contracts: Contractual and Noncontractual Remedies' in L DiMatteo, M Cannarsa and C Poncibò (eds), *The Cambridge Handbook of Smart Contracts, Blockchain Technology and Digital Platforms* (Cambridge University Press 2019) 121.

[50]A Guadamuz, 'All watched over by machines of loving grace: A critical look at smart contracts' (2019) 35 Computer Law and Security Review 11.

[51]Clifford Chance and EBRD, 'Smart Contracts: Legal Framework and Proposed Guidelines For Lawmakers' (2018) 30; J Erbguth, 'Transparenz von Smart Contracts' in M Fries and B Paal (eds) *Smart Contracts* (Mohr Siebeck 2019) 25, 33.

Moreover, there is always the possibility that the technological integrity of the system is compromised.

If the smart contract coding is integrated with AI systems, there is the black-box problem[52] along with other problems of consumer protection such as the availability of pre-contractual information rights, or the possibility of using a right of withdrawal from a smart contract.[53] These black-boxes prevent consumers from fully understanding the technical logical structure adopted by AI during the course of smart contracts since algorithms are only readable or understandable by software developers and programmers.[54] According to Stacy-Ann Elvy, AI-enhanced smart contracts could worsen the power imbalance and information asymmetry in consumer contracts by growing the contractual distance between consumers and the other party.[55]

Third, there can be some problems depending on the type of smart contract. There are different types of smart contracts. Some smart contracts are the translation of natural language agreements into code. These are used to automatically execute the terms of a contract that the parties have previously concluded in natural languages (off-chain SC).[56] Some smart contracts on the other hand are comprised solely of code. These create new contractual relationships that are both defined and executed automatically by code (on-chain SC/solely encoded SC).[57] In on-chain smart contracts, the rights and obligations of the parties are written in coding language.[58] Contractual matters that are not included in the computer code do not become a part of the parties' agreements.[59] These different types of smart contracts require different legal considerations.[60] In the case of solely encoded smart contracts, there is the difficulty of establishing the intention

---

[52] Algorithms are kept by the organisations that created them or are so complex that even their creators cannot explain how they work. AI's 'black box' problem can be described as the inability to see through what is inside an algorithm. WD Eggers and M Turley, 'The future of regulation: Principles for regulating emerging technologies' <https://www2.deloitte.com/us/en/insights/industry/public-sector/future-of-regulation/regulating-emerging-technology.html> accessed 25 January 2023.

[53] For the consumer protection issues regarding smart contracts see, M Durovic and C Willett, 'A Legal Framework for Using Smart Contracts in Consumer Contracts: Machines as Servants, not Masters' (2023) 86 Modern Law Review 1309; L Forbes, 'Consumer Protection in the Face of Smart Contracts' (2022) 34(1) Loyola Consumer Law Review 45; O Borgogno, 'Usefulness and Dangers of Smart Contracts in Consumer Transactions' in DiMatteo, Cannarsa and Poncibò (n 49) 288.

[54] A recent article in CoinDesk points out that 'tokenization and smart contracts – two vital components of the blockchain ecosystem – are also witnessing increased integration of AI. However, the black box problem can obscure the logic behind AI-generated tokens or smart contract execution.' See S Jagati, AI's black box problem: Challenges and solutions for a transparent future (*cointelegraph*, 5 May 2023) https://cointelegraph.com/news/ai-s-black-box-problem-challenges-and-solutions-for-a-transparent-future accessed 5 June 2023.

[55] SA Elvy, 'Contracting in the Age of the Internet of Things: Article 2 of the UCC and Beyond' (2015–2016) 44 Hofstra L. Rev. 839.

[56] S Green, 'Smart Contracts: Interpretation and Rectification' (2018) Lloyd's Maritime and Commercial Law Quarterly 234, 238; E Théocharidi, 'La conclusion des smart contracts: révolution ou simple adaptation?' (2018) 161 Revue Lamy droit civil 48, 52.

[57] Also see UK Law Commission: A solely code smart contract is a smart legal contract in which all the contractual terms are defined in, and performed automatically by, the code of a computer program. UK Law Commission, 'Smart Contracts Advice to Government' (2021) https://lawcom.gov.uk/project/smart-contracts/.

[58] Clifford Chance (n 51) 12; F Möslein, 'Smart Contracts im Zivil- und Handelsrecht' (2019) 183(2–3) Zeitschrift für das gesamte Handelsrecht und Wirtschaftsrecht 254, 264; M Demeyer, 'Blockchain Technology and Smart Contracts from a Financial Law Perspective' (LLM thesis, University of Gent 2018) 84 https://pdfs.semanticscholar.org/0109/b04d3115a126340acb8ffd74dc0e92fdea00.pdf, accessed 25 January 2023.

[59] J Lingwall and R Mogallapu, 'Should Code Be Law: Smart Contracts, Blockchain and Boilerplate' (2019) 88(2) University of Missouri-Kansas City Law Review 285, 299.

[60] According to the results of the consultation carried out by the UK Law Commission, 'natural language contracts with automated performance are most commonly used in practice. However, some consultees, expressed the view that the use of hybrid and solely code smart legal contracts have potential too. We believe that regulatory clarification would lead to the uptake of solely encoded smart contracts'. UK Law Commission (n 57) at 26.

to create legal relations. In these smart contracts, there is no natural language interaction between the parties and the contract is formed by conduct. In order to assess whether parties to an on-chain smart contract intended to create legal relations, several factors can be taken into account including the nature and purpose of the platform on which the code is deployed, or the nature of the transactions executed by the smart contract code.[61] The parties most of the time cannot verify in the beginning, whether the smart contract will do what it promised to do or not. The off-chain smart contract can also be a cause for dispute. In the case of off-chain smart contracts, it is difficult to fully reflect the intentions of the parties in code and the translation from natural language to code is prone to mistakes.[62]

Another point of conflict arises from the immutable nature of smart contracts. Smart contracts are performed as coded. Even though the circumstances surrounding the conclusion of the contract change, due to the automation and self-enforcing nature, the smart contract will be executed no matter what. The *pacta sunt servanda* principle is strictly adhered with.[63] Unless expressly coded, smart contracts cannot take the changing circumstances into account.[64] This means for instance that it is not possible to update the conditions for a long-term trade relationship.

Oracles, which are independent computer programmes that feed data outside the blockchain into the smart contract might also lead to disputes between smart contract parties.[65] A person, a programme or a website can act as an oracle, i.e. it can provide information from the outside world to the smart contract.[66] For example, an online service can provide stock exchange rates or currency exchange rates. Smart contracts cannot verify whether an oracle has provided correct information.[67] Especially when humans are acting as oracles, the data provided to the smart contract may not be real or accurate. Therefore, oracles do not have the reliability feature of the blockchain.[68] They also have negative impacts on the reliability and security of smart contracts by offering a point of entry.

When using smart contracts, the lack of legal capacity of parties is easily hidden from the blockchain.[69] Public blockchains do not perform controls for checking legal capacity, therefore, anyone can open an account even if they lack capacity. From a legal perspective, certain categories of persons, such as those under a certain age, those who lack mental capacity or those who are incapacitated cannot enter into legally binding agreements. Even if one of the parties does not have the legal capacity to act, the transaction

[61] UK Law Commission (n 57) 56.

[62] ibid 104–05.

[63] RH Weber, 'Smart Contracts and What the Blockchain has got to do with ıt?' in M DesStefano and G Dobrauz-Saldapenna (eds), *New Suits Appetite for Disruption in the Legal World* (Stämpfli 2019) 35 at 367; M Cannarsa, 'Contract Interpretation' in DiMatteo, Cannarsa and Poncibò (n 49) 111.

[64] UK Law Commission (n 57) 139–40.

[65] P Cuccuru, 'Beyond Bitcoin: An Early Overview on Smart Contracts' (2017) 25(3) International Journal of Law and Information Technology 179, 186;, Werbach and Cornell (n 6) 336; M Kaulartz and J Heckmann, 'Smart Contracts- Anwendungen der Blockchain Technologie' (2016) 32(9) Computer und Recht 618, 620; J Grimmelmann, 'All Smart Contracts Are Ambiguous' (2019) 2(1) Pennysylvania Journal of Law and Innovation 1, 14.

[66] S Legner, 'Smart Consumer Contracts – Die automatisierte Abwicklung von Verbraucherverträgen' (2021) 1 Verbraucher und Recht 10, 15.

[67] T Kuntz, 'Konsens statt Recht? Überlegungen zu Chancen und Herausforderungen der Blockchain-Technologie aus juristischer Sicht'(2020) 220(1) Archiv für die Civilistische Praxis 51, 78.

[68] E Mik, 'Smart Contracts: Terminology, Technical Limitations and Real-World Complexity' (2017) 8 LIT 1, 296.

[69] B Ancel, 'Les smart contracts: revolution sociétale ou nouvelle boîte de Pandore ? Regard comparatiste' (2018) (7-8) Communication Commerce électronique 15, 17.

performed by that person through the smart contract will be executed automatically when the conditions stipulated in the smart contract are fulfilled. In this case, after the transaction has taken place, a separate lawsuit must be filed, and the transaction must be marked as invalid in an *ex-post* manner.[70]

As it can be seen from the examples given above, there are some matters that may result in the invalidity or modification of the smart contract. Due to the deficiencies and mistakes surrounding the formation of smart contracts, one or both parties might need to resort to the right to challenge the offer or acceptance expressed via smart contracts. The deficiencies can also lead parties to use the right to cancel, revoke or withdraw from the contract or claim for damages. In some cases, stopping or suspension of the automatic execution of the smart contract or reversal of its performance will be in the interest of the parties.[71] One thing that is valid for each jurisdiction is that disputes regarding smart contracts will mostly arise after the contract is executed. Smart contracts change the emphasis of the remedy from performance to restitution. It is expected that the use of smart contracts will potentially cause a rise in restitution claims and damages.[72]

The next question is this: Do the legal systems need to deal with these matters by resorting to new regulations? Or are the existing laws and regulatory frameworks sufficient to deal with the complications arising from the use of smart contracts?

D. Regulatory perspectives

Emerging technologies such as artificial intelligence, big data, internet of things, DLT and its applications have the potential to cause economic and legal disruptions. They create new ways for consumers to interact.[73] They are no doubt a challenge to existing legal taxonomies.

Most jurisdictions have already implemented regulatory frameworks focusing on the financial aspects of crypto asset related transactions.[74] They are mostly focused on consumer protection, market integrity, and AML/KYC obligations. Some states in the USA (Wyoming, Tennessee, Vermont) have implemented new legislation on DAOs[75] which determine the character of the entity and some issues like governance structure and liability.[76] The EU has adopted MiCA (Markets in Crypto Assets) which focuses on bringing

[70] J Schrey and T Thalhofer, 'Rechtliche Aspekte der Blockchain' 2017 (20) Neue Juristische Wochenschrift 1431; T Hoffman and V Skwarek, 'Blockchain, Smart Contracts und Recht, Smart Contracts als Risiko für Informatiker' (2019) 42(1) Informatik Spektrum 197, 201.

[71] Clifford Chance (n 51).

[72] R Herian, 'Legal Recognition of Blockchain Registries and Smart Contracts' EU Blockchain Observatory and Forum (2018) 18 http://oro.open.ac.uk/59481/9/Legal%20Recognition%20of%20Blockchain%20Registries%20and%20Smart%20Contracts%20%28Final%20Draft%20Report%20%2B%20Appendix%29.pdf accessed 25 January 2023.

[73] Eggers and Turley (n 52).

[74] J Ellul and others, 'Regulating Blockchain, DLT and Smart Contracts: A Technology Regulator's Perspective' (2020) 21 (209) ERA Forum 210: 'Approaches have included outright bans of cryptocurrencies and Initial Coin Offerings (ICOs), using a case-by-case vetting and approval process of such activities, and clear guidelines regarding whether a particular activity can operate and eventually receive regulatory approval.'

[75] J Teague, 'Starting a DAO in the USA? Steer Clear of DAO Legislation A Primer on DAO Legislation in Multiple States' https://thedefiant.io/starting-a-dao-in-the-usa-steer-clear-of-dao-legislation> accessed 25 January 2023.

[76] According to a report newly published by the EU Blockchain Observatory and Forum, 'efforts are underway to better understand how DAOs work when it comes to contract law and how to address contributor liability. In addition, jurisdictional banking, tax, and employment compliance requirements are unclear. Questions remain regarding the applicability of existing laws and corporate entity forms, versus the creation of entirely new and legally recognized forms.' EU Blockchain Observatory and Forum (n 24) 24.

crypto-assets, crypto-assets issuers, and crypto-asset service providers under a regulatory framework.

What about smart contracts? Is a new regulatory regime needed for smart contracts? This is a tough question since the problems arising from smart contracts concern many areas of law. These include – but are not limited to – contract law, property law, tax law, company law, private international law, data protection law, and consumer protection law.

It can be seen that there are different regulatory approaches when it comes to smart contracts.[77]

I. A primer: can code be a regulatory instrument?

Considering the high number of interactions currently being governed by software, smart contracts that guarantee performance as programmed can be used as regulatory tools. For instance, it is possible to design regulatory obligations directly into technological products. Accordingly, smart contracts can be used to define rules[78] and act as means or tools that directly enforce rules in an effective way.[79]

As more contractual provisions start being implemented in the form of a smart contract, the blockchain (and smart contracts) acquires the status of a 'regulatory technology'. The rules defined in the smart contract can be enforced irrespective of whether there is an underlying legal rule or not.[80] In this scenario, governments can experiment with new means of code-based regulation to achieve specific policy goals.[81] They can ensure compliance[82] by relying on these code-based systems which make sure that rules and regulations are automatically enforced.[83] This means that the government no longer has to monitor each and every transaction.[84]

To be effective, these blockchain-based solutions need to be adopted by private parties. The government on the other hand must enact laws and regulations to mandate that regulated institutions and other private parties interact with these code-based systems. De Filippi and Wright have asserted that new laws could necessitate that banks and other financial institutions interact with a government-backed smart contract or other code-based systems whenever they perform money transfers. This would safeguard compliance with the law on money transmission.[85]

Regulators could require parties to loans to input maximum interest rates to prevent usury and monitor for compliance. Smart contracts can also be used in the consumer protection realm. They can self-enforce potential contractual disputes and incorporate pro-consumer terms (such as the right of cancellation and claims for compensation).

[77] For an overview of possible regulatory approaches for DLT-based activities, see: M Finck, *Blockchain Regulation and Governance in Europe* (Cambridge University Press 2018) 11; G Gabison, 'Policy Considerations for the Blockchain Public and Private Applications' (2017) 19 SMU Science and Technology Law Review 327.

[78] Finck (n 77) 14.

[79] P De Filippi and S Hassan, 'Blockchain Technology as a Regulatory Technology: From Code is Law to Law is Code' (2016) 21(12) First Monday 1, 2.

[80] ibid 15.

[81] P De Filippi and A Wright, *Blockchain and the Law* (Harvard University Press 2018) 193.

[82] ibid 197.

[83] EU Blockchain and Observatory Forum (n 24) 27.

[84] De Filippi and Wright (n 81) 196.

[85] ibid 199.

A smart contract code may, for instance, embody the European passenger rights and automatically refund money to consumers in the event of a delay or cancellation.[86]

The EU Blockchain Observatory and Forum has reported that 'from today's perspective, smart contracts that represent digital assets can – and should – be written in such a way as to make them regulatory compliant'.[87] On 12 October 2022, the Saudi Communications and Information Technology Commission (CITC) published a whitepaper addressing the role of blockchain technology as a regulatory tool.[88] According to the Whitepaper, regulations will be translated into executable smart contracts and regulated entities will record any performed operation into the distributed ledger.

II. The 'wait and see' approach

In the smart contract realm, most jurisdictions have endorsed the 'wait and see' approach. This approach allows regulators to understand the technology, observe how the technology evolves, and how the use cases develop without taking any regulatory action. During this phase, existing regulations are maintained.[89]

For instance, the Federal Reserve (the Central Bank in the USA) indicated in 2016 that the technology requires 'much more complex demonstrations in real-world situations before these technologies can be safely deployed in today's highly interconnected, synchronised and far-reaching financial markets'.[90] In the same stance, in 2018 Swiss Federal Council has expressed their take on smart contracts specifically as:

> parties wishing to conclude a smart contract should provide for suitable mechanisms for possibly changing circumstances and dispute resolution. There will certainly be further developments around smart contracts, but as it is still in the embryonic stage, *it seems premature to legislate at the moment.*[91] (emphasis added)

In the EU, the Digital Finance Package introduced a proposed regulation on markets in crypto-assets (MiCA), published in the Official Journal of the EU in June 2023.[92] It was a first step towards creating a legal governance structure for crypto assets. With regard to smart contracts on the other hand, the regulation is silent. Smart contracts are only mentioned in the EU regulatory framework in the Data Act, which was proposed by the European Commission on 23 February 2022, only indirectly. Regarding DAOs, which utilise smart contracts for functioning, the EU Blockchain and Observatory Forum in

[86] D Roumpos, 'Liability of The Smart Contract Developer. A Comparative Analysis in the light of US and EU Law' (2020) 42 http://arno.uvt.nl/show.cgi?fid=152251 accessed 25 January 2023.

[87] EU Blockchain Observatory and Forum (n 24) 27.

[88] 'Blockchain as a Regulatory Tool' (October 2022) 22 https://www.cst.gov.sa/ar/research-innovation/Documents/BlockchainasaRegulatoryTool.pdf, accessed 25 January 2023.

[89] World Bank Group, 'How Regulators Respond to Fintech Evaluating the Different Approaches – Sandboxes and Beyond' (2020) Finance, Competitiveness & Innovation Global Practice Fintech Note No. 538, 38.

[90] 'Fed's Brainard sees Blockchain as Revolutionary, But Still to Prove Itself' (*Reuters*, 7 October 2016) https://www.reuters.com/article/us-usa-fed-brainard-idINKCN1272BG accessed 25 January 2023.

[91] Swiss Federal Council (n 35) 81.

[92] On 24 September 2020 the European Commission published a legislative proposal for a regulation on markets in crypto assets (MiCA). The main aim is to clarify the application of existing EU rules to crypto-assets, and to allow operators authorised in one Member State to provide their services across the EU. MiCA lays down several safeguards including capital requirements, custody of assets, complaint handling processes, and common disclosure standards for the issuance of Initial Coin Offerings (ICOs). Proposal for a Regulation of the European Parliament and of the Council on Markets in Crypto-assets and amending Directive (EU) 2019/1937, COM(2020). It is expected that MiCA will come into force in 2024 the latest.

their recent report have stated that: 'When it comes to legal and regulation, we are in very early days. DAOs are currently not categorised as specific legal entities in most parts of the world, which makes for rather opaque regulatory enforcement. Efforts are underway to better understand how DAOs work when it comes to contract law and how to address contributor liability'.[93] It seems that smart contractual aspects will not be dealt with soon in the EU.

It is true that a better understanding of technological and economic developments as well as possible regulatory shortcomings is crucial before regulations on blockchain, and its applications can be advanced.[94] The wait and see approach may satisfy economic and ideological demands in the immediate term. However, in the long-term legal certainty and clarity are risked. Moreover, the jurisdictions run the risk of not being able to offer verdicts that correctly assess the conflicting interests of the parties where the smart contract is not concluded properly or there is a breach of contract.[95] Hence there are risks associated with this approach such as risks around contractual fairness, consumer protection, security vulnerabilities and financial stability.[96]

III. The decision not to regulate

Another option is not to change the existing legal framework. One of the reasons why the jurisdictions might follow this path is that blockchain technology is advancing faster than law. This pace of technology leaves reactionary legislation for those creating and transacting with smart contracts, DAOs and NFTs futile. Traditional legal systems are mostly political and slow to act. Furthermore, since smart contract transactions can involve parties from different countries, hence more than one jurisdiction, regulations need to be international and gain extensive acceptance.[97]

According to some authors especially commenting on the common law systems, the existing contractual and commercial regulations already have the advantage of being flexible enough to be integrated with adequate tests elaborated by the courts. Therefore, case law is the most 'technology neutral' tool to regulate and demystify technology, including smart contracts.[98]

The primary risk associated with not regulating smart contracts at all is losing clarity and legal certainty. If smart contracts are not regulated, this means that their functioning and effects are left to public policy decisions or the advancement of technology. This can push away stakeholders in the sector who might fear that 'operating within such a jurisdiction could impose risks that can be mitigated by moving to a jurisdiction with a regulatory framework in place'.[99] It is indicated in the above-mentioned surveys that,[100] the

---

[93]EU Blockchain Observatory and Forum (n 24) at 23.
[94]Swiss Federal Council (n 35) 43.
[95]Herian (n 72) 30. According to Mouton, regulators should consider smart contract's effects on the financial intermediary sector because doing nothing causes a gap in law and uncertainty for market participants. J Mouton, 'Regulating Smart Contracts in the Domain of Financial Trading'(2021) 57 Cal. W. L. Rev. 441, 463.
[96]World Bank Group (n 89) 38.
[97]WA Kaal and C Calcaterra, 'Crypto Transaction Dispute Resolution' (2018) 73 BUS. LAW. 1, 45–46.
[98]M Dell'Erba, 'Demystifying Technology. Do Smart Contracts Require a New Legal Framework? Regulatory Fragmentation, Self-Regulation, Public Regulation' (17 May 2018) 49, available at SSRN: https://ssrn.com/abstract=3228445 or http://dx.dxoi.org/10.2139/ssrn.3228445, accessed 25 January 2023.
[99]Ellul and others (n 74) 210.
[100]See (n 45).

lack of regulatory clarity is one of the main barriers to the widespread adoption of smart contracts. In order to spur innovation, providing at least guiding principles ensuring consumer protection and citizens' rights, and providing safeguards against anti-competitive practices is necessary.[101]

It should be underlined that even if regulators decide that smart contracts should not be regulated at all, it does not mean that they will function within in a legal vacuum.[102] One of the main benefits of smart contracts is that they enable disintermediation to a degree, but they cannot eliminate all intermediaries from a contract or economic activity. Contracts and economic activity cannot be isolated from history, norms, law, regulations, and governance institutions that determine their framework and constrain an activity. Therefore, the parties to a smart contract cannot interact with one another with total autonomy on a peer-to-peer basis.[103] There is and will still be some conflicts around the formation, interpretation, and performance of smart contracts. Smart contracts do not prevent fraud, illegality, or unconscionability in the formation process:

> If a human makes a mistake in contracting by smart contract, the law of mistake should be applied. If the automated system encounters an un-codeable event of force majeure, impossibility, impracticability, or frustration of purpose, then those doctrines ought to apply to contracts automatically executed by computers through decentralized ledgers just as they apply to contracts automatically executed by any other means.[104]

When such conflicts arise, then it is for the lawyers to decide how they fit into the existing regulatory frameworks.

Before reaching the decision not to regulate, the regulators should first review the current legislative and regulatory framework to decide if amendments to existing laws may be required or desirable to better facilitate the use of smart contracts. The regulators should make sure if there are some implications of smart contracts that current law does not allow. Surely, the existing legal framework will change from jurisdiction to jurisdiction. But in general, the existing legal provisions on consumer protection,[105] protection of personal data,[106] liability of platform operators, applicable law, intellectual property rights and dispute resolution should all be considered. In many jurisdictions, laws on electronic transactions can act as the basis for determining the regulatory framework for smart contracts. The existing contract law framework will also be applied to smart contracts to decide on the meeting of minds, control of standard contract terms, formal requirements, and interpretation. It is also important that parties who interact with smart contracts in certain industries must comply with the law and regulations that are applicable and specific to that industry. Know your customer ('KYC') and Anti Money-Laundering (AML) requirements are examples of these obligations.

---

[101] EU Blockchain and Observatory Forum, 'Legal and Regulatory Framework of Blockchains and Smart Contracts' (2019) 10 https://www.eublockchainforum.eu/sites/default/files/reports/report_legal_v1.0.pdf accessed 25 January 2023.

[102] De Filippi and Wright (n 81) 78.

[103] Lehr (n 41) 18.

[104] J Fairfield and N Selvadurai, 'Governing the Interface Between Natural and Formal Language in Smart Contracts' (2022) UCLA J.L. & Tech. 79, 117.

[105] EU Unfair Terms Directive 93/13/EEC, Unfair Commercial Practices Directive 2005/29/EC and Consumer Rights Directive 2011/83/EU.

[106] In the EU for instance, it is important that the use of smart contracts fulfil the requirements for the protection of personal data laid down in the General Data Protection Regulation 2016/679. See, WG Voss, 'Data Protection Issues for Smart Contracts', in M Corrales Compagnucci, M Fenwick and S Wrbka (eds) *Smart Contracts: Technological, Business and Legal Perspectives* (Hart 2021) 79–100.

The UK is one of the countries that has reached a decision not to regulate smart contracts after thorough consideration. As a country keen on being a leader in the blockchain ecosystem, the UK has been focusing on how the existing rules apply to smart contracts. Already in 2019, Sir Geoffrey Vos stated that: 'We should try to avoid the creation of a new legal and regulatory regime that will discourage the use of new technologies rather than provide the foundation for them to flourish'.[107] As a first step, in November 2019, UKJT published a legal statement on crypto assets and smart contracts.[108] In this legal statement, the UKJT concluded that in principle, smart contracts could give rise to binding legal obligations, enforceable in accordance with their terms. Next, the Ministry of Justice asked the Law Commission to undertake a detailed analysis of the current law as it applies to smart legal contracts and to highlight any uncertainties or gaps and identify such further work as may be required then or in the future. In this framework, they have also consulted with participants in the ecosystem with a call for evidence to identify areas of uncertainty where reform may be required.[109] In 2021, the Law Commission published an Advice to Government based on the response they received to the call for evidence. In the document, it was stated that the current legal framework in the UK was sufficiently robust and adaptable to facilitate and support the use of smart legal contracts. They also underlined the fact that the flexibility of common law meant that the jurisdiction of England and Wales provided an ideal platform for business and innovation, without the need for statutory reform.[110]

IV. Decision to regulate

Finally, the jurisdictions can choose to regulate smart contracts and address the issues arising from their use specifically. They can opt for the establishment of ex ante regulatory frameworks through which smart contracts can emerge and develop. This approach has some advantages too. When lawmakers engage in active discussion and legislative efforts to statutorily recognise smart contracts, they demonstrate their eagerness to embrace new technologies.[111] A clear regulatory framework would provide consumer protection mechanisms to investors and stakeholders. At the same time, imposing obligations on operators could help combat illegal activity.[112] According to Herian, 'Claims that regulations will stifle innovation need only consider whether innovation has, until now, been stifled by existing laws and regulations, with smart regulation that works closely with innovation as the bare minimum standard required'.[113] The EU Blockchain Observatory and Forum also draws attention to the importance of regulation:

> If blockchain-enabled markets are to mature, policy makers and businesses must create the rules of engagement together. Regulators should provide guiding principles to attract

[107] G Vos, 'Cryptoassets as Property: How Can English Law Boost the Confidence of Would-be Parties to Smart Legal Contracts?' (2 May 2019) Joint Northern Chancery Bar Association and University of Liverpool Lecture, https://www.judiciary.uk/wp-content/uploads/2019/05/Sir-Geoffrey-Vos-Chancellor-of-the-HighCourt-speech-on-cryptoassets-2.pdf accessed 25 January 2023.

[108] UK Jurisdiction Taskforce, 'Legal statement on cryptoassets and smart contracts' (November 2019) <https://resources.lawtechuk.io/files/4.%20Cryptoasset%20and%20Smart%20Contract%20Statement.pdf≥ accessed 25 January 2023.

[109] UK Law Commission, 'Smart Contracts Call for Evidence'.

[110] UK Law Commission (n 57).

[111] Arcari (n 39) 379.

[112] Ellul and others (n 74) 210.

[113] Herian (n 72) 7.

> private-sector investors, ensure consumer protection and citizens' rights, and provide safeguards against anticompetitive practices.[114]

Currently an international, uniform regulatory regime focusing on smart contracts does not exist.[115] We should start by emphasising that smart contracts are not easy to regulate. This challenge is not specific to smart contracts and indeed a common feature of all newly emerging technologies. Technology evolves faster than regulation or social structures governing them.[116] It is tricky to define and identify the practices and related products and services which are newly implemented by various institutions.

Since smart contracts are written and stored on the blockchain, they share the characteristics such as anonymity or pseudo-anonymity of parties. Moreover, the smart contract ecosystem is transnational. The parties involved in a smart contract transaction, such as the parties, code developers, miners, platform operators may be subject to different regulatory regimes.[117] The fact that it is difficult to know who is using the platform and to what end makes it even more complicated to police or regulate smart contracts.[118] 'With the need to attribute liability, certify transactions, and reconcile these technologies with data protection imperatives creates critical challenges for governments'.[119]

In addition to all this, not all regulators can understand the nuances of distributed ledger technology. The EU Blockchain Observatory and Forum has approached this point from an identity management perspective. They indicated that

> as authorities, including regulators and the courts, become more aware and knowledgeable about blockchain, they will be in a better position to evaluate whether blockchain-based timestamping solutions can qualify under the eIDAS framework. We believe they should be enabled and encouraged to continue to deepen their understanding in this area.[120]

These two aspects taken together draws attention to one thing: The nature and characteristics of smart contract transactions make cross-jurisdictional harmonisation important. This means that regulators and lawmakers across national borders must collaborate to harmonise legal and regulatory regimes.[121] Addressing the issues arising from smart contracts would require a good level of knowledge on the working principles and use cases. Having a well-founded mechanism to ensure alignment is also significant since the process will possibly end up with legal and organisational changes having an impact globally.

There are some countries who have provided some level of legal clarification for smart contracts. In Europe, Italy and Belarus have opted for defining smart contracts. In the USA, there has been a combination of all the regulatory approaches. Some states have opted for legislation, such as Arizona, Nevada, Tennessee, etc. Some have endorsed the wait and

---

[114] EU Blockchain Observatory and Forum (v 1.0) 7 https://www.eublockchainforum.eu/sites/default/files/reports/report_legal_v1.0.pdf, accessed 25 January 2023.

[115] According to Lehr, risks associated with finance and the challenges of addressing them existed long before smart contracts emerged and there are long-established regulatory institutions and approaches for managing these issues. Therefore, smart contracts do not need separate regulation. Lehr (n 41) at 26.

[116] M Amaral, 'Blockchain and smart contracts: regulatory challenges and regulatory approaches' in *OECD Case Studies on the Regulatory Challenges Raised by Innovation and the Regulatory Responses* (OECD Publishing 2021)

[117] ibid.

[118] EU Blockchain and Observatory Forum (n 24) 10.

[119] Amaral (n 116).

[120] EU Blockchain and Observatory Forum (n 24) 12.

[121] ibid 13.

see approach. Some governmental bodies in the USA, just like the UK, has underlined the risks of over-regulation for innovation. In 2018, ESRA and the Chamber of Digital Commerce published a joint statement in response to the states which opted for regulation and enacted legislation on smart contracts.[122] They have stated that legislation seeking to define smart contracts or ensure that smart contracts are legally enforceable, while well-intentioned might be harmful. This is due to several reasons: First, different definitions on smart contracts might be confusing for the courts. Second, in the USA, there are existing federal regulations which can also be applied to smart contracts such as the Electronic Signatures in Global and National Commerce Act ('ESIGN Act') or Uniform Electronic Transactions Act ('UETA'). These acts regulate and authorise the use of electronic signatures and they already provide a sufficient legal foundation for the enforcement of smart contracts as well.[123] They can sufficiently encompass the digital 'signatures' obtained in smart contract transactions and therefore remove the need for any further state action to recognise and adopt smart contracts. Accordingly, additional state legislation would create inconsistent and unnecessary state laws which would hinder innovation.

In the next part, we will discuss what the focus of smart contracts regulations should be, if the authorities decide that smart contracts should be regulated.

E. The 'how' and 'what' of smart contract regulation

There are two steps that should be followed when there is a decision to regulate smart contracts.

First, the regulatory goals should be determined by taking into account the interest of the parties involved in a smart contract transaction: Who are the actors in the smart contract ecosystem? What are their interests and how/why does a conflict of interest occur? The next step should be striking a balance between these competing interests. When striking this balance, the regulators will aim for supporting innovation, promoting competition and economic growth and on the other side, they will try to mitigate unacceptable financial risks for consumers and investors. The law makers should focus on all the possible actors who engage with smart contracts technology such as the developers, designers, users, consumers, data providers etc.[124] Possible new roles and responsibilities will also have to be dealt with by regulators. Should regulators bring some limits on the permitted use of certain smart contracts? Should regulatory authorities be given access to distributed ledgers – such as in smart consumer contracts?

One of the most important parts surrounding the debate around the regulation of smart contracts is deciding about 'what' should be regulated. It can be seen from the wide range of books, articles, reports, and projects dedicated to smart contracts that there are some problematic areas that must be dealt with as primary areas of concern. We will elaborate on them one by one in this part of the article.

---

[122]Joint Statement in Response to State Smart Contracts Legislation https://esignrecords.org/wp-content/uploads/2018/04/Joint-Ltr-State-Smart-Contracts-Legislation.pdf accessed 25 January 2023.

[123]For detailed information regarding the regulation of smart Contracts under (UETA), (ESIGN), and (UCITA), see Dell'Erba (n 98) 27.

[124]Herian (n 72) 29.

I. Defining smart contracts

The initial and basic regulatory move is to provide a definition for smart contracts. Including a smart contract definition in the regulatory framework has the advantage of providing legal clarity. Some countries have endorsed this approach. Belarus was the first country to define smart contracts in a Presidential Decree as: 'a programme code intended for functioning in the distributed ledger for purposes of automated performance and/or execution of transactions or performance of other legal actions.[125] Italy was the first European country that regulated 'smart contracts' and introduced a definition. In the law titled 'On urgent provisions regarding the support and simplification of the business system and public administration' smart contract is defined as: 'a computer program based on distributed registry technologies, the use of which is legally determined by two or more parties based on previously concluded agreements'.[126]

In the USA some states such as Tennessee, Arizona, Wyoming, and Nevada have already passed laws on smart contracts.[127] These laws cover a narrow framework of a clarificatory nature that provides definitions on smart contracts and guarantee their enforceability rather than making radical changes.[128] Some authors believe that legislature stepping in at an early stage and clarifying basic questions is helpful because 'until smart contracts come before the courts, the courts cannot declare on their own accord that smart contracts are enforceable and if so on what terms'.[129] Some authors, on the other hand are of the opinion that these laws 'demonstrate a premature accommodation of smart contracts and an incomplete attempt to predict the future of technological development'.[130]

The European Law Institute which is an independent non-profit organisation established to initiate, conduct and facilitate research, make recommendations, and provide practical guidance in the field of European legal development also commenced a project on Blockchain Technology, Smart Contracts and Consumer Protection in 2018. The team elaborated a list of principles to support legislators in drafting sets of specific rules that are more appropriate to contracts in this field whenever such a derogation from traditional contract law is fitting. The project also had the aim to help judges in their roles as interpreters of the resulting legislation. In the Principles formulated by the ELI, a definition of smart contract was introduced: 'Computer program that, upon the occurrence of pre-defined conditions, runs automatically and executes pre-defined actions'.[131]

---

[125] Decree of the President of the Republic of Belarus No. 8 (21 December 2017), unofficial translation.

[126] Law n.12/2019 published in the Gazzetta Ufficiale on February 12, 2019, Simplification Law, in article 8-ter paragraph 3.

[127] For detailed information regarding the legislation, Ferreira (n 4) at 9-12.

[128] ibid 12.

[129] In the USA, there still needs to be a decision made: Will there be regulations on a state level or a uniform code? It should be mentioned that The Uniform Law Commission and the American Law Institute created a committee- investigating how smart contracts should be treated under the UCC. See E McDonald, 'Smart Contracts' (5 November 2021), <https://journals.library.columbia.edu/index.php/CBLR/announcement/view/445> accessed 20 May 2023.

[130] For criticism of state-level legislation in the USA see M Orcutt, 'States That Are Passing Laws to Govern 'Smart Contracts' Have No Idea What They're Doing' (2018) MIT Tech. R. https://www.technologyreview.com/s/610718/states-that-are-passing-laws-to-govern-smart-contracts-have-no-idea-what-theyre-doing/ accessed 25 January 2023; J Madir, 'Smart Contracts' in J Madir (ed), *Fintech Law and Regulation* (Elgar 2021) 177.

[131] European Law Institute, 'ELI Principles on Blockchain Technology, Smart Contracts and Consumer Protection' (2023) 14 https://www.europeanlawinstitute.eu/fileadmin/user_upload/p_eli/Publications/ELI_Principles_on_Blockchain_Technology__Smart_Contracts_and_Consumer_Protection.pdf, accessed 25 January 2023.

II. Termination and unwinding of smart contracts

When the smart contract is verified and recorded on the blockchain, the code and result of the smart contract transaction is recorded irrevocably. Therefore, the transaction cannot be changed, stopped or reversed. Even if the smart contract is comprised of lines of code that contain reasons of invalidity according to the reasons stipulated in the legal rules of (the applicable) law, the smart contract will continue to self-enforce. The smart contracts that do not comply with formal requirements or those that are void or voidable based on a lack of contractual capacity will be automatically enforced as well.[132] The same goes for smart contracts where the performance of the smart contract violates public policy or advocates criminal activity. Since the smart contract cannot detect these anomalies, it cannot stop the automatic execution.

If the smart contract code is executed despite the legal flaws and the parties are unhappy with the outcome of the smart contract, they would need to wait for the smart contract to complete execution and then seek legal redress. In this case, the courts must decide, in an ex-post manner, that the outcome realised by the implementation of the smart contract, is null and void.[133] This is not enough for the unwinding of the contract and bringing the parties to the status quo ante. To provide the status quo ante in smart contracts, the other party must agree to perform a refund by making a new transaction. Therefore, it will be useful to discuss how alternative solutions can be brought to eliminate the incompatibility between the legal order and the blockchain.

To align the situation in blockchain and the legal order, it is technically possible to go back to a former state of blockchain by using 'reverse transactions'. A reverse transaction does not enable the deletion of the transaction history or any specific transaction. In this case, the status of a transaction is updated and corrected by a later transaction. With this new transaction, it is possible to show the cancellation and its legal consequences by referring to the original transaction that is intended to be cancelled.[134]

As it can be seen from the scenarios provided above, smart contracts are expected to give rise to post-execution cases where the court must decide if contract performance should be reversed. Therefore, regulators need to focus on what is optimal or desirable for their own jurisdictions on the burden of proof structure implied in post-execution cases.[135]

One solution to this problem would be to enable a termination button ('kill-switch') in the smart contract to stop its execution. 'A 'kill switch' allows the parties to step out of the smart contract. If activated, the smart contract stops operating and the parties can determine the appropriate course without interference by technology'.[136] 'Killing' or 'self-destructing' the original smart contract and then directing users to the address of the

---

[132] The Chancery Bar Association and Commercial Bar Association (joint response) said that it may be necessary to impose legal limitations on who may have access to a private key or who may sign a transaction on a DLT system, to safeguard the interests of parties who lack capacity. UK Law Commission (n 57) 45.

[133] L DiMatteo, M Cannarsa and C Poncibò, 'Smart Contracts and Contract Law' in DiMatteo, Cannarsa and Poncibò (n 49) 12.

[134] U Bertram, 'Smart Contracts, Praxisrelevante Fragen zu Vertragsabschluss, Leistungsstörungen und Auslegung' (2018) 23 Monatsschrift für Deutsches Recht 1416, 1420; R Lupu, 'Herausforderungen und Lösungsansätze bei der Gestaltung von Blockchain-basierten Smart Contracts' (2019) 35(10) Computer Recht 631, 633.

[135] World Bank Group (n 89) at 21.

[136] S Farrell, H Glass, and H Wells, 'Practice Makes... Pragmatic Designing a Practical Smart Contract Legal Architecture' in Allen and Hunn (n 11) 353, 366. According to the authors 'Building practical safeguards into the technology at the outset places control of the commercial arrangement in the hands of the parties, not the technologists. Safeguards

new smart contract could be achievable.[137] Using this function, the parties can use their right to bail out and if necessary, pay the penalty before the smart contract is executed. The parties to the smart contract should wisely design the circumstances in which a party should be able to resort to the kill function. This would also avoid the problem of determining damages concretely at the time of conclusion of the contract.[138] Another solution would be creating a code that can address the failure of the smart contract.[139]

These mechanisms can be regulated to provide clarity and certainty. An example for regulating the termination of smart contracts can be seen in the EU. As mentioned above, the EU had endorsed the wait-and-see approach for quite a long time. The first legislative act concerning smart contracts was the EU Data Act. On 23 February 2022, the European Commission published its proposal to harmonise rules on fair access to and use of data. Smart contracts are considered to be useful in facilitating smooth data sharing and offering effective technical protection of the data and the underlying database. According to the Data Act, smart contracts must have internal functions which can reset the contract or stop its further execution, ('safe termination and interruption'). The Data Act however, does not address, who should have the power to demand such actions and under which circumstances.

Unwinding by a reverse transaction is recognised under ELI Principle 10. According to this principle, 'where the applicable law provides for the unwinding of a transaction, such unwinding shall normally occur by a reverse transaction unless the blockchain at hand allows for the modification of blocks'.[140] Although this sounds promising in principle, we believe that the elements and mechanisms for reverse transactions also call for regulation.

III. Use of oracles

Oracles are another area of concern that will surely fall into the regulatory radar. When there is a smart contract that depends on extrinsic data to be triggered,[141] the trustworthiness of the oracle is significant for the contract to be executed correctly. Oracles, however, are data sources external to blockchain[142] whose accuracy and timeliness is not guaranteed. They carry the risk of being compromised and feeding the blockchain with false information ('the oracle problem'). Especially in situations where the information provided by the oracles are not verifiable by the agents, trustworthiness becomes more fundamental.[143] The oracle problem can hinder smart contract design and implementation.

---

allow parties to take advantage of smart contract technology, secure in the knowledge that the parties will be able to achieve the right commercial result, even if the technology does not operate as intended.' at 367.

[137] Also see T Schrepel, *Smart Contracts and the Digital Single Market Through the Lens of a 'Law + Technology' Approach* (Publications Office of the European Union 2021).

[138] O Meyer, 'Stopping the Unstoppable: Termination and Unwinding of Smart Contracts' (2020) 9(1) Journal of European Consumer and Market Law 23.

[139] ibid 24.

[140] European Law Institute (n 131) 41.

[141] Chainlink, What Is the Blockchain Oracle Problem? (*Chainlink*, 27 August 2020) https://blog.chain.link/what-is-the-blockchain-oracle-problem/ accessed 25 January 2023: 'Financial smart contracts need market information to determine settlements, insurance smart contracts need IoT and web data to make decisions on policy payouts, trade finance contracts need trade documents and digital signatures to know when to release payments, and many smart contracts want to settle in fiat currency on a traditional payment network.'

[142] Mik (n 68).

[143] Giulio Caldarelli. 2020. 'Understanding the Blockchain Oracle Problem: A Call for Action' (2020) Information 11, no. 11 509.

The UK Law Commission, in the 'Smart Legal Contracts: Advice to Government', has identified oracles as one of the new issues and risks that the legal system would need to respond to. According to the Law Commission, oracles may require further consideration or indeed regulation.[144] In the same document, the views provided by the ecosystem participants is also shared. According to the Chancery Bar Association and Commercial Bar Association, the reliance of smart legal contracts on oracles may entail the 'shifting of trust to oracles or arbitrators who are brought in to resolve disputes', rather than entirely removing the need for trust. These associations predicted that the regulation of oracles and other intermediaries will be an important issue.[145]

IV. Allocation of liability

Allocation of liability is another problematic issue that can be addressed. Most of the time, the parties to a smart contract do not have the technical expertise to draft and deploy the smart contract code. Therefore, they rely on a smart contract model provided by an individual coder or coders developing the smart contract code.[146] We have stated in this article repeatedly that correct performance in accordance with the parties' intentions cannot be guaranteed. There is always the risk that smart contract code will be hacked or that it contains a programming or design error resulting in cyberattacks, token thefts, and data manipulations.[147] When coding errors and resulting cyber-attacks occur, smart contract developer(s) may be exposed to liability towards the parties.

The questions about liability in smart contracts are manifold: Who will be held liable for failure of execution or partial execution due to technical flaws or malfunction? Who will be held liable for operational defects, corrupted messages, or defective programme logic? Who will be held liable if an oracle does not feed correct data to smart contracts? Is it possible to attribute liability in cases where parties use open-source software? To what extent and under which conditions can the developer of the code[148] that contains the errors or bugs be held liable?[149] In case the smart contract is audited and certified, should the auditor be liable?

It is apparent that the 'parties to a smart contract will need to consider how risk and liability for unintended coding errors and resulting exploitations are allocated between the parties, and possibly with any third-party developers or insurers of the smart contract'.[150] A challenge while determining smart contract liability is that there are many parties involved and determining the dynamics of the relationship between them is difficult.[151]

---

[144] UK Law Commission (n 57) 6.
[145] ibid 22.
[146] Roumpos (n 86) 44.
[147] ibid 52.
[148] In October 2018, Brian Quintenz, Commissioner of the Commodity Futures Trading Commission, suggested that smart contract code developers could be held accountable for aiding and abetting CFTC violations where they 'could reasonably foresee, at the time they created the code, that it would likely be used by U.S. persons in a manner violative of CFTC regulations'. Remarks at the 38th Annual GITEX Technology Week Conference (16 October 2018) <https://www.cftc.gov/pressroom/speechestestimony/opaquintenze16> accessed 25 January 2023.
[149] Clifford Chance (n 51) at 31.
[150] SD Levi and AB Lipton, 'An Introduction to Smart Contracts and Their Potential and Inherent Limitations' (2018) https://corpgov.law.harvard.edu/2018/05/26/an-introduction-to-smart-contracts-and-their-potential-and-inherent-limitations/ accessed 25 January 2023.
[151] Madir (n 130) 191.

Lawmakers have several choices on the issue: They may require that the parties to the smart contract specifically address the issue of allocation of liability. Or they can empower certain authorities such as financial services regulators to make rules on liability allocation for smart contracts. Especially in the case of smart contracts with consumers, lawmakers could provide that the non-consumer party will be held liable in the event of any bugs in the code, incorrect performance of the software, etc. They can even mandate that this allocation of liability would override any conflicting term in the contract itself.[152] According to Borselli, 'joint and several liability should be imposed on insurance companies and third-party providers for damages due to flaws and discrepancies in the smart contract code and algorithms'.[153]

V. Smart contract libraries

Ever since the potential of smart contracts were realised, there is also the issue of developing a library of smart contract code. There are many open-source smart contract libraries available that provide reusable building blocks for a project.[154] Accordingly, smart contract developers can find reusable behaviours that can be added to the smart contracts and implementations of various standards in smart contract libraries.[155]

Thanks to smart contract libraries, the smart contract in a transaction does not need to be written from scratch every time. When there is a ready-to-use smart contract, there is no need for re-coding which saves time. Moreover, since open-source smart contract libraries are inspected thoroughly by the community, the possibility of finding errors is lowered. It should also be mentioned that some smart contract libraries undergo external audits for additional security.[156]

Lawmakers or regulators can create rules on developing smart contract templates, which could include a field for the parties to indicate their agreement regarding how liability will be allocated in the event of a coding error. It might even be possible to provide a warning message in cases where the parties did not expressly agree on allocation of liability for a coding error.[157]

VI. Consumer protection in smart consumer contracts

Another area that has been widely discussed both for use cases of distributed ledger technology in general and specifically for smart contracts is consumer protection. Currently smart contracts are mostly used for B2B transactions; however, they are also functional and relevant for B2C transactions as well. Although B2C smart contracts are not common yet,[158] technology is advancing fast, and consumers are becoming more acquainted with distance contracts in e-commerce especially after the Covid-19 pandemic. According to the report of the UK Law Commission, smart contracts automate

[152]Clifford Chance, (n 51) at 32.
[153]Borselli (n 40) 121.
[154]Smart Contract Libraries (15 August 2022), https://ethereum.org/en/developers/docs/smart-contracts/libraries/ accessed 25 January 2023.
[155]ibid
[156]ibid.
[157]Clifford Chance (n 51) at 35.
[158]According to Durovic and Willett 'SCs do have potential to be more broadly used in B2C contracts' (n 53) 1397.

the delivery of photographs to consumers and in 'ride-sharing' contracts.[159] And we see new potential use cases of smart contracts every day. Therefore, it is sensible to determine the risks and potential efficiency advantages for the consumers considering the radical changes smart contracts can bring to contractual performance and enforcement.[160]

When electronic contracts became common use, consumers needed to be given adequate legal protection in the digital realm. After the emergence of smart contracts, the issue of consumer protection needs to be revisited. Applying the consumer protection rules designated for electronic contracts to smart consumer contracts would not yield satisfactory results.[161] Due to their unique characteristics, smart contracts require a more specific framework.

Once the consumer protection mechanisms are observed, it can be seen that consumers are usually granted informational rights, cooling-off periods, protection against unfair terms and right to revoke or withdraw from the contract within a designated time frame.[162] Implementing these rights and obligations on an immutable, automated blockchain network is a challenge. Automated contracting through smart contracts might reverse the burden of proof to the consumer's disadvantage. Retailers would simply receive the payment automatically through smart contract execution, and consumers would bear the burden of proof if they claimed that such payment should not have been made.[163]

According to Brownsword, 'the use of smart contracts in the consumer marketplace is likely to be one of the hot spots for regulatory debate and, possibly, the sharing economy will give rise to some questions about an acceptable balance of interests'.[164] If the regulatory path is followed, there are some points that need to be carefully considered in the consumer protection realm.

First, who the consumer is needs to be determined by considering the transnational and peer-to-peer character of smart contract transactions. Since smart contract transactions occur in an algorithmic environment, classical consumer protection concepts will not suffice. In smart contracts, consumers are not protected against a business with a stronger bargaining power but they are protected against a P2P (peer-to-peer) platform.[165] While determining who the consumer is, the nature of the transaction, the sector and the geographic location also have significance. It is also important to determine what kind of transactions would be covered by a regulation and if there is going to be a value threshold.

Second, there are several factors that need to be taken into consideration when dealing with consumer protection. On one hand, smart contracts make it easier and faster for consumers to make transactions without being subjected to excessive formalities. On the other hand, consumer understanding of the nature of smart contracts

[159] UK Law Commission (n 57), para 6.33-6.34.
[160] Durovic and Willett (n 53) 1392.
[161] For the differences between the concept of electronic contracts and smart contracts, see Möslein (n 58) 261. For instance smart contracts allow for the application of more complex rules and enforcement mechanisms. They do not need intervention from humans to perform. Werbach and Cornell (n 6) 321; R De Caria, 'The Legal Meaning of Smart Contracts' (2019) 6 European Review of Private Law 731, 736.
[162] M Kloth, 'Blockchain basierte Smart Contracts im Lichte des Verbraucherrechts' (2022) Verbraucher und Recht 214, 217.
[163] EU Blockchain Observatory and Forum (n 24) 13.
[164] R Brownsword, 'Smart Contracts: Coding the Transaction, Decoding the Legal Debates' in P Hacker and others (eds), *Regulating Blockchain: Techno-Social and Legal Challenges* (Oxford University Press 2019) 323.
[165] ELI Principles (n 131) 40.

is low. Since the algorithmic nature of smart contracts can be less transparent and controllable than a classical electronic transaction, consumers' vulnerability is a point for consideration.[166] Therefore, there must be some mechanisms designed to balance the pros and cons for the consumers. We believe that denying the existence of a contractual relationship is not feasible, therefore regulations must be placed to ensure that consumers still enjoy protection as in off-chain contracts. According to Durovic and Willett, it is possible to merge some consumer protection values with the logic of a smart contract. This is true for information and cooling off rights. A smart contract can even make the exercise of cancellation rights more efficient.[167] But some consumer rights that are time-sensitive and complex in the sense that they require complicated legal analysis are harder to be integrated with smart contract. For instance, especially long-term B2C contracts can lead to problems when consumers face lack of conformity or an unfair term related problem. Taking these possibilities into account, the parties can encode for the possibility to pause a long-term smart contract and direct the issue to ADR for analysis and reasoning, which would suspend the obligations of the consumer.[168] This makes it more effective for consumers since they do not have to make formal application for the initiation of an ADR process. However, they also highlight that,

> *It must surely be the law that mandates*[169] that long-term B2C contracts only use SC technology capable of being paused for human/ADR intervention, and then restarted to deliver on what has been agreed by the humans. Ideally this should be done by specific rules that provide precisely that this must happen.

Following up on the previous point, an alternative dispute resolution mechanism specific to smart consumer contracts can be designed to ensure that consumer can have a recourse mechanism when things go wrong. It is of utmost importance that this mechanism is understood by the consumer.

In the ELI Principles, it is established that *even greater protection is needed for consumers on-chain than off-chain.* It is laid down in Principle 15 that '*Agreements regarding the use of programming language cannot be concluded between businesses and consumers. Smart contracts used for consumers always have to be translated into natural language.*[170] This principle in a way limits the use of solely encoded smart contracts in consumer transactions.

The ELI principles also include a separate rule regarding the right to a cooling-off period encoded into the smart contract. Moreover, the principles foresee that the smart contract shall be programmed in such a way that when a consumer exercises their right of withdrawal, the exercise of such right by itself results in a reverse transaction, taking into consideration the nature of the performance. If the nature of the performance prevents a reverse transaction, the consumer may be entitled to a monetary claim representing the value of the transaction.[171]

---

[166]ibid 30.
[167]Durovic and Willett (n 53) 1405.
[168]ibid 1412.
[169]Emphasis added.
[170]ELI Principles (n 131) 51.
[171]ibid 47.

VII. Smart contract dispute resolution

Blockchains operate globally and they enable participants in multiple jurisdictions to transact with each other. The parties to a smart contract can be anonymous. Hence, when the parties and courts are dealing with smart contract disputes, the first issue that they need to tackle is the choice of law and jurisdiction: Who to sue, where to sue them and which law will be applied?[172]

There can be some mechanisms such as ex-ante coding some functions to avoid breaches. However, there will always be new problems that are unaccounted for or unforeseeable which results in technical and legal problems. Besides, traditional litigation fails to address smart contracts' need for remedies that preserve anonymity and fit within the blockchain. Smart contract disputes cannot be resolved by resorting to traditional courts and traditional processes since they simply will not work for resolving smart contract and NFT disputes.[173] According to Sir Geoffrey Vos, in order to ensure legal certainty and investor protection, there should be

> a built-in species of dispute resolution specifically designed for smart contracts, so as to ensure a legal infrastructure for future contracting parties. I am thinking of an expedited dispute resolution process entrenched in the code itself, which would allow ultimately for ADR, arbitration or judicial resolution.[174]

There are some initiatives that deal specifically with smart contract dispute resolution. JAMS is the first institutional ADR provider to create protocols supporting the use of ADR in disputes arising from blockchain activities, including smart contracts.[175] UKJT has published Digital Dispute Resolution Rules for arbitrations of digital disputes, facilitating arbitration in a blockchain and Smart Contract based environment.[176] According to Arcari, the UETA in the USA should be amended to require parties to submit disputes to dispute resolution proceedings or arbitration hearings to efficiently and conclusively provide contracting parties with tools to resolve dispute.[177]

ELI has recognised the rules regarding choice of law and choice of forum to be applied to smart contracts.[178] It was highlighted in another report that, lawmakers should determine if existing laws permit parties to refer disputes arising from smart contracts to arbitration. It was also emphasised that lawmakers should also determine whether decisions arising from existing dispute resolution mechanisms (such as court judgments) could be reflected directly in the smart contract by becoming a supported data source or oracle input for DLT-based smart contracts. Regulators should also consider how judgments may be published and utilised by smart contract systems.[179]

---

[172] Arcari (n 39) 394. If the parties to a smart contract have not made an express arrangement regarding their choice of law which location will be taken into account to decide about which law will govern the contract: The location of the participants to the transaction? The location of the relevant asset? The location of software? Madir (n 130) 194.

[173] AJ Schmitz, 'Resolving NFT and Smart Contract Disputes' in N Geslevich Packin (ed), *The Cambridge Handbook on the Law and Policy of NFTs* (Cambridge University Press forthcoming).

[174] Vos (n 11) 68.

[175] JAMS, JAMS Smart Contract Clause and Rules (DRAFT), https://www.jamsadr.com/rules-smart-contracts accessed 25 January 2023.

[176] UK Jurisdiction Taskforce, 'Digital Dispute Resolution Rules' (2021) https://resources.lawtechuk.io/files/2.%20UKJT%20Digital%20Disupte%20Rules.pdf accessed 25 January 2023.

[177] Arcari (n 39) 395.

[178] ELI Principles (n 131) 50.

[179] Clifford Chance (n 51) 46.

VIII. Smart contract code audit

The auditability of the smart contract code is another area of regulatory concern.[180] There is no doubt that blockchain technology is secure and reliable. However, blockchain applications such as smart contracts have security vulnerabilities.[181] There are various reasons why technical errors exist in smart contracts – such as the developer's incapacity to understand the complex programming language and properly create secured algorithms; the inaction, negligence, or swiftness of the coder.[182] It should be underlined that it is not easy to find out that bugs have exploited the code of the smart contract.

Since smart contracts are susceptible to risks, it is important to discover errors, bugs and security vulnerabilities in the smart contract code. Otherwise, the vulnerabilities in the code are open to attacks or malicious manipulation of the smart contracts' content. Unfortunate incidents, especially form the financial sector, such as the cyber-attacks of 'Mt. Gox' and 'Bitstamp' Bitcoin exchanges, demonstrate that smart contracts can be hacked and prove that cyber-security is an important issue facing smart contracts.

Interoperability, certainty, flexibility, accountability, and safety are significant when designing a smart contract code. Parties wishing to transact using smart contracts should take into consideration the security of their smart contract code and carefully audit it or have it audited before deploying it. Code that is written incorrectly or tested inadequately can expose the smart contract to security threats. For instance, unauthorised parties can be able to trigger or otherwise interact with the smart contracts which will result in undesired outcomes.

In a smart contract audit, a detailed analysis of the contract's code is carried out to ensure correct operation prior to deployment. This can identify security issues and incorrect and inefficient coding and help to determine ways to resolve the problems.[183] Developer support tools can help to reduce errors while writing the smart contract code. Testing can be carried out by independent mechanisms and in the future, it is expected that this kind of audit can be aided by AI systems.

The EU Legal and Regulatory Framework on Blockchain and Smart Contracts has underlined the need for quality assurance and technology audit processes:

> Audits help test your smart contracts for immunity to various attacks, due to issues like timestamp dependence, weak protocol code, and malicious external calls. It is also essential to get audits conducted after updates to test smart contracts for all errors and issue a report with identified vulnerabilities and improvement recommendations.[184]

The issue of security of the smart contract code is revisited in the EU Data Act as well. It is stated that smart contracts must offer a high degree of protection against functional errors and manipulation by third parties; that is they should be robust. Moreover, it must be possible to archive transactional data, the smart contract logic, and code to keep a record of the operations performed on the data in the past of a terminated

---

[180] OECD (n 10) 12.
[181] 'What is a smart contract audit' https://hedera.com/learning/smart-contracts/smart-contract-audit#:~:text=A%20smart%20contract%20audit%20involves,and%20reliability%20of%20blockchain%20applications accessed 25 January 2023.
[182] Roumpos (n 86) 38.
[183] 'What is a Smart Contract Audit' (n 181).
[184] EU Blockchain Observatory and Forum (n 24) 10.

smart contract. This is to ensure auditability as well as for data archiving and continuity purposes.

According to Salazar, courts and regulators can be supplemented with mandatory corporate auditing of smart contracts with regard to bias, discrimination, data privacy breaches and technical failures. Placing companies under more public and regulatory scrutiny may encourage them to remove unfair terms and conditions along with bias, discrimination, and technical failures in their smart contracts.[185] Companies can be required to disclose the auditing results in order for regulators and the general public to monitor the fairness of smart contracts.[186]

IX. Smart contracts and formal requirements

Since smart contracts became popular, the following question has been asked again and again: Can a smart contract, which is in a nutshell a piece of computer code, satisfy the in-writing requirement in contracts? It is generally accepted that a written contract does not have to be natural language prose. It is rather important to establish the intention of the parties. Therefore, smart contracts should not be treated in a less advantageous way than other forms of electronic records. But can the cryptographic key with which smart contracts are signed using asymmetric public-private key encryption, be considered 'electronic signatures'?[187]

'Digital Signatures' are the mathematical scheme for exhibiting the authenticity of electronic signatures and electronic records using asymmetric cryptography. When we look at the EU, eIDAS is the EU Regulation which aims to harmonise the regulation of electronic signatures and transactions to build and ensure trust in these signatures and to ensure the safety of online business opportunities and transfers of electronic funds. This model is based on a central certification authority. These authorities issue and revoke the certificates based on strict protocol. This means that although the signatures that are used to formulate a smart contract are functionally equivalent to the PKI model-based electronic signatures as regulated by eIDAS, they (public-private keys) remain automatically excluded from being 'qualified electronic signatures' due to the centralised trust system built into the regulation.[188] ELI Principles (Nr. 7) address the issue of formal validity.[189] Accordingly,

> Formal requirements, such as the requirement that a contract must be in writing and signed, or needs to be drawn up in a particular format, such as an (authentic) deed, can only be

[185] V Salazar and R Alberto, 'Unconscionability, Smart Contracts, and Blockchain Technology: Are Consumers Really Protected against Power Abuses in the Digital Economy?' (2021) 9 International Journal on Consumer Law and Practice 74, 76.

[186] ibid 92–93.

[187] Another aspect with regard to formal requirements in smart contracts is the role of third parties taking part in transactions to validate and verify. According to Madir, 'as a matter of public policy, lawmakers will need to consider whether the role of such third parties as notaries should be retained or may be automated. This will, to a large extent, depend on the role that such third parties play in the transaction process, that is, whether their role is limited to identifying parties or is broader and involves warning the parties about the implications of the contract they are entering into'. See Madir (n 130) 191.

[188] A Veerpalu and others, 'The Hybrid Smart Contract Agreement Challenge to European Electronic Signature Regulation' (2020) 28 International Journal of Law and Information Technology 39, 78. The authors suggest to amend eIDAS to include 'functional equivalence' clauses to allow also decentralised protocol-based key generation and management, and various alternative ways to fulfil the identification function than just the CA-centric PKI model, at 83.

[189] ELI Principles (n 131) 40.

> fulfilled by a blockchain transaction or a smart contract if the algorithmic representation of a written contract or deed equivalent to the off-chain use of such requirements: (1) guarantees the same safeguards; and (2) accomplishes the purpose of such formal requirements; and (3) regarding electronic signatures, fulfils the requirements of the electronic Identification, Authentication and trust Services (eIDAS) or an equivalent regulatory framework.

The regulators need to establish the standards as to when blockchain signatures constitute qualified electronic signature.

In the USA some states' regulators made specific legislation regarding the form of smart contract and its signature in a smart contract-specific legal act. The same approach was endorsed by Italy. Italian laws state that 'smart contracts meet the requirement of written form following the computer identification of the interested parties, through a process having the requisites set by the Agency for Digital Italy with guidelines to be adopted'[190] These guidelines have not been published yet. The smart contract regulations in the USA and Italy qualifies the smart contract as either a contract in electronic form or written form.

X. Smart contracts and modification

A smart contract cannot be deleted or altered once deployed. But the parties to smart contracts will continue to disagree about the terms governing their performance and how the smart contract was intended to operate. However, unlike traditional contracts, it is not possible to amend the smart contract code to reflect changes in the underlying circumstances surrounding the arrangement, to correct errors, or to reflect changes in law.[191] The need for modification increases as smart contracts interact with outside data. Considering all these possibilities, the ability to change smart contracts a critical factor in enabling smart contracts to operate in a practicable way.[192]

Since blockchain is immutable there are several ways that can be used to create an effect similar to modifying a smart contract. Ex-ante solutions are often used in practice to enable smart contracts to be modified similarly to adapting the contract to changing circumstances. Incorporation of oracles and kill switch features into smart contracts, as well as deciding on online dispute resolution methods can be used at this stage.[193] At the same time, parties can take advantage of artificial intelligence or the technical remedies Ethereum provides, such as self-destruct, to modify their smart contracts.[194] These problems can also be overcome by opting for private and permissioned blockchain networks or by using hybrid contracts, which can provide a smoother transition to smart contracts instead of solely encoded smart contracts.[195]

---

[190] Art 8-ter(2) DL 135/2018 of 14 December 2018, converted into law by Law 12/2019 of 11 February 2019.

[191] Madir (n 130) 197.

[192] Herian (n 72) 22.

[193] JI-H Hsiao, "Smart' Contract on the Blockchain-Paradigm Shift for Contract Law?' (2017) 14 US-China Law Review 690; E Tjong Tjin Tai, 'Challenges of Smart Contracts- Implementing Excuses' in DiMatteo, Cannarsa and Poncibò (n 49) 80; L Efimova, O Sizemova and A Chirkov, 'Smart Contracts: Between Freedom and Strict Legal Regulation' (2021) 30 Information and Communications Technology Law 333, 345; T Xu, 'Smart Contracts: The Limits of Autonomous Performance' in Allen and Hunn (n 11) 23; C Morgan, D Livingston and A Moir, 'Dispute Resolution for the Digital Economy' in Allen and Hunn (n 11) 437.

[194] H Nguyen and S Bailey, 'Use of Artificial Intelligence for Smart Contracts and Blockchains' (2018) 21 FinTech Law Report 1.

[195] E Mik, 'Blockchains-A Technology for Decentralized Marketplaces' in DiMatteo, Cannarsa and Poncibò (n 49) 172.

It is possible to find ways to modify the relationship executed by a smart contract. But should this be regulated by the lawmakers? Under Tennessee Law, smart contracts used in the management of a DAO must be capable of modification or amendment.[196] According to an author, the UETA should be added new provisions to enable modification. First, errors must be reversible by request of either party by completing a reversed transaction. Second, any such reversal should be recorded on the same blockchain where the original transaction occurred.[197]

XI. Data privacy in smart contracts

Smart contract deployment in a variety of financial products and services will require wide-ranging connections with data sources. Some authors highlight the fact that 'most current smart contract and blockchain platforms lack privacy-preserving mechanisms, especially for transactional privacy'.[198] Governments, standard setting bodies, and international organisations could establish task forces to identify types of data widely used in smart contracts, develop standards for ensuring data reliability and transparency, and designing platforms for data dissemination.[199]

F. Conclusion

With blockchain and its new applications, regulators around the world are going through a tricky time trying to balance conflicting interests. The same occurred when the internet became widespread, and an increasing number of people started contracting via electronic contracts. These contracts are widely used now. And they did not require major changes in the existing laws in the sense of a reform. Regulators have been comfortable with many regulated transactions transitioning to purely electronic form.[200] We tried to address if the same can be achieved for smart contracts. We believe that legal systems will adapt to these innovations incrementally.[201]

With the advancements in technology, the level of automation will increase, and the burden of enforcement will shift to code. However, code is not law and regulatory oversight will always be necessary. Formation, interpretation and execution of smart contract code will require a new regulatory approach and skillset. A successful integration of reasonable regulation and smart contracts could provide both regulators and stakeholders with significant efficiencies in compliance. In order for smart contracts to accomplish their true potential, smart contracts 'have to become flexible to accommodate the contractual safeguards incorporated in an appropriately developed body of laws to address real-world issues such as tech failures, attacks, war/natural disasters, crime, tax,

---

[196]Amendment No. 1 to HB2645.

[197]Arcari (n 39) 394.

[198]Z Zheng, S Xie, H-N Dai and others, 'An Overview on Smart Contracts: Challenges, Advances and Platforms' (2020) 105 Future Generation Computer Systems' 475, 482.

[199]World Bank Group, 'Finance, Competitiveness & Innovation Global Practice Fintech Note, No. 6' (2020) 21.

[200]Chamber of Digital Commerce (n 3) at 40.

[201]Ferreira (n 4) 15. Also see, Justice A Abdullah and Y Goh, 'Making Smart Contracts a Reality: Confronting Definitions, Enforceability, and Regulation' in Allen and Hunn (n 11) 78: ' … clarificatory attempts should not too radically change the law. After all, as we have briefly canvassed, traditional contract law can be applied to smart contracts with little modification. It would cause too much uncertainty if statutes were designed to upend that stability.'

and changing legislation to enhance adaptability'.[202] To gain investor confidence which is crucial in increasing the use of smart contracts, investors need to be able to resort to legal remedies for instance to avoid fraud and rely on a dependable market.[203] For instance, if regulators design laws concerning consumer financial products that use smart contracts, then the efficiency of funds can increase and consumer protection can be ensured for the investors.[204]

It is best for regulators to first understand the functioning of the technology using regulatory sandboxes and identify their potential risks and legal issues. Then it should be considered, how the regulatory framework can be adjusted without hindering innovation. Considering the global nature of smart contracts there is a need for uniform standards of regulation – at least international unified set of standards[205] as complementary rules to contractual laws – to avoid possible risks of regulatory arbitrage. Although the 'no new regulation' approach has the undoubtable advantage of simplicity, regulators could run the risk of nullifying the aspects of blockchain that are truly innovative while they are 'squeezing a new phenomenon into old requirement'[206] The regulators are currently not feeling the urge to address smart contracts, since the general public's smart-contract use is minimal. But it should also be considered that remaining inactive on smart contract regulation can result in misuse of smart contracts in ways that are not anticipated by the regulators.[207]

Disclosure statement

No potential conflict of interest was reported by the author(s).

Funding

This research was supported by TÜBİTAK (The Scientific and Technological Research Council of Türkiye).

[202]EU Blockchain Observatory and Forum (n 24) 11.
[203]Vos (n 11) 57.
[204]Mouton (n 95) at 465.
[205]T Kadour Aleinieh and L Zoboli, 'Increasing Standardization for Smart(Er) Contracts' (2021) Unif. L. Rev. 1, 13.
[206]EU Blockchain Observatory Forum (n 24) 33.
[207]Mouton (n 95) at 465.

Is the syndicated loans market ready for distributed ledger technology?

Hüseyin Can Aksoy

ABSTRACT
The syndicated loan market has a centralised nature dominated by intermediaries. Such a structure not only requires manual labour and back-office workloads, but it is also prone to human error and fraud. Distributed ledger technology (DLT) and smart contracts are promising tools to overcome the factors which adversely affect the efficiency of the current and classical business model in the primary and secondary market of syndicated loans. DLT eliminates the need for intermediaries; provides transparency, accuracy, and authenticity; lowers transaction costs; makes it easier to comply with Know Your Customer obligations; and provides efficiency in the secondary market for syndicated loans. However, existing legal rules and institutions fail to create a predictable and legally safe environment for the spread of DLT in the syndicated loans market. Therefore, proper regulation is required for the widespread use of DLT technology in the syndicated loan market.

A. Introduction

Today, financing of large-scale investments such as dams, power plants and telecommunication services are generally provided by credit consortia, also known as syndications, formed by several lenders. In such method of financing, more than one independent institution establishes a temporary partnership to provide a certain financing transaction, and each of these institutions undertakes to provide a certain percentage of the total loan needed by the borrower.

Syndicated loan market has a centralised nature, which is dominated by intermediaries, who act as a bridge between the lenders and the borrower, keep information on centralised databases, and carry out the clearing and settlement concerning the loan. Loan documents are in PDF format and amendments are usually distributed by email. Such structure not only requires manual labour and back-office workloads but it is also prone to human-error and fraud.

Distributed ledger technology ('DLT') and smart contracts are seen as significant tools to overcome these factors, which adversely affect the efficiency of the current and classical business model in the *primary* and *secondary market* of syndicated loans. Use of DLT could ease the negotiation, execution, administration and trading of loans in the syndicated loan markets.[1]

In 2018, a Spanish bank and its two partner banks completed the first syndicated loan transaction on the blockchain. The underwritten loan amount was 150 million euro and the entire negotiation took place on a private blockchain network.[2] The network was secured by user codes and information was time-stamped to show the exact time of each event's occurrence.[3] The use of blockchain technology also provided full document tracking and transparency.[4]

Despite all the advantages of DLT and smart contracts, existing legal rules and institutions fail to create a predictable and legally safe environment for the spread of DLT in the syndicated loans market. In this paper, I will elaborate on the potential advantages that DLT and smart contracts can offer in the syndicated loans market, and make public policy recommendations for utilising such benefits to the fullest extent.

In this paper, I will firstly explain the features of syndicated loans. Secondly, I will elaborate on the use of DLT in the syndicated loans market. After defining the concepts of distributed ledger, blockchain and smart contracts, I will discuss the advantages of using DLT for the syndicated lending actors. Current literature generally focuses on how DLT would contribute to the syndicated loans market. However, there are many drawbacks that cannot be overcome without proper legal intervention. Therefore, in the last section of the paper, I will elaborate on the drawbacks that need to be addressed and the need for proper regulation.

B. Syndicated loans: an overview

A syndicated loan is a loan supply in which multiple credit institutions are involved on the lender's side, thereby sharing the risk of non-repayment of the loan.[5] The syndicated loan market was created by banks that have limited financial resources to meet financial needs of their high-profile customers. By coming together, separate banks are able to meet the needs of their customers under the same terms and conditions.[6]

Through joint documentation, participants of the syndicate meet the borrower's large loan demand under the same terms and conditions. In this framework, each lender in the syndication undertakes to provide a certain portion of the total loan and in return has the same right to the repayments made by the borrower.[7] Participants could trade their loan receivables in the secondary market.

[1] D Petrov, 'The Impact of Blockchain and Distributed Ledger Technology' [2019] International Scientific Journal Industry 4.0 88, at 90.

[2] For detailed information about this transaction, see L Gonzalez-Echenique, 'Blockchain: The Future of Syndicated Lending?' [2019] Butterworths Journal of International Banking and Financial Law 326, 326.

[3] L Noonan, 'Banks complete first syndicated loan on blockchain' (*Financial Times*, 6 November 2018) <https://www.ft.com/content/2b12d338-e1d1-11e8-a6e5-792428919cee> accessed 28 January 2023.

[4] P Martino, *Blockchain and Banking: How Technological Innovations Are Shaping the Banking Industry* (Springer 2021) 41.

[5] K Simons, 'Why Do Banks Syndicate Loans?' [1993] New England Economic Review 45, 45; A Fight, *Syndicated Lending* (Elsevier 2004) 1; J Ho, 'Chapter 2 – Basic Principles of Syndicated Lending: Financing Through the Risk Spectrum' in A Shutter (ed), *A Practitioner's Guide to Syndicated Lending* (Sweet & Maxwell 2017) 9.

[6] Fight (n 5) 2.

[7] W Wild, 'The Economic Basis of Syndicated Lending' (PhD thesis, Queensland University of Technology 2004) 1; CE Aster and MA Attaway, 'Syndicated Construction Loans, Defaulting Lenders, and Equitable Remedies' [2016] Texas Tech Law Review 853, 859.

Syndicated loans are procured under the leadership of a credit institution called 'consortium leader' or 'lead bank'. The first step in procuring a syndicated loan is for the borrower to apply to a bank that will act as the 'lead bank' for a certain fee.[8] The lead bank may be the bank that will provide the highest amount of credit to the borrower within the syndication, or it may be an institution preferred by the borrower as it has sufficient influence in the market in terms of establishing the syndication.[9] It is also possible that the lead bank is a bank that has a long established business relationship with the borrower.[10]

The main task of the lead bank is to ensure the establishment of syndicate by interviewing potential lenders. The lead bank also negotiates the terms of the loan agreement with the borrower.[11] After the syndication is established, the borrower usually only deals with the lead bank.[12] It is common to decide that the loan amount provided by the lenders will be transferred to the borrower through the leading bank.[13] In accordance with the terms of a consortium agreement to be signed among the lenders, it is also among the duties of the leading bank to re-distribute these payments among the lenders.[14] The lead bank is responsible in keeping all information on centralised databases.[15] Syndicated lending has several advantages both for the lenders and the borrowers. In the international banking sector, non-repayment of loans is one of the main reasons that cause financial difficulties for credit institutions.[16] With the provision of loans through syndication, the risk of non-repayment of the loan is shared among the lenders. Another function of syndicated loan is to diversify the loan portfolios of banks.[17] The lead bank meets the needs of its customers and receives a fee for this service, without supplying the entire loan itself.[18] In fact, one of the reasons that push banks to share loan supply with other banks through syndication is legal restrictions on capital.[19] It is undesirable for a bank to lend by risking a large part of its resources.[20] In addition, the possibility of the loan receivables to change hands in the second-hand market eliminates the risk of concentrating the bank's resources on a single borrower.[21] Syndicated loans also provide significant benefits to the borrowers. This method eliminates the need for the borrower to negotiate a loan with more than one bank and overcomes the problems of obtaining loans from different banks under different

---

[8]DZ Nirenberg, 'International Loan Syndications: The Next Security' [1984] Columbia Journal of Transnational Law 155, 159.

[9]ME Jones, 'Bankers Beware: The Risks of Syndicated Credits' [1999] North Carolina Banking Institute 169, 173.

[10]ibid 173.

[11]PR Pollock, 'Notes Issued in Syndicated Loans – A New Test to Define Securities' [1977] The Business Lawyer 537, 538.

[12]Wild (n 7) 25; GA Goodman, 'Special Problems of Syndicated Loans' (*Dentons*, 14 April 2014) 4 <https://www.dentons.com/en/insights/articles/2014/april/14/special-problems-of-syndicated-loans> accessed 28 January 2023.

[13]MHughes, 'Transferability in Syndicated Lending' [2007] Law and Financial Markets Review 21, 21.

[14]Wild (n 7) at 25.

[15]D Petrov, 'A New Digital Age in Finance: Blockchain and Smart Contracts' [2020] Horizons: International Scientific Journal 7, 9.

[16]I Callaghan, 'Chapter 10 – Making the Loan: the Theory and Mechanics of Syndicated Lending' in Shutter (n 5) 189.

[17]Simons (n 5) 45; LB Gutcho, 'Syndicated Lending: Lead Banks and Syndicate Members' [1994] International Business Lawyer 131, at 131; Jones (n 9) 177; SA Dennis and DJ Mullineaux, 'Syndicated Loans' [2000] Journal of Financial Intermediation 404, at 408; V Ivashina and Z Sun, 'Institutional stock trading on loan market information' [2011] Journal of Financial Economics 284, 284.

[18]Nirenberg (n 8) 161; Goodman (n 12) 2.

[19]Simons (n 5) at 45; Dennis and Mullineaux (n 17) at 407; Jones (n 9) 177.

[20]Aster and Attaway (n 7) at 858.

[21]Simons (n 5) at 46.

conditions.[22] In addition, since the borrower meets all his loan needs with a single loan contract, the transaction cost of the borrower is reduced.[23]

Despite all the benefits the syndicated loan provides for the actors of the syndicated lending, the syndicated loans market is dominated by intermediaries. This not only increases transactions costs but also causes concerns about the transparency, accuracy and authenticity of the transactions. In this regard, DLT and smart contracts are seen as significant tools to ease the negotiation, execution, administration and trading of loans in the syndicated loan markets. In the next section, I will elaborate on the use of DLT in syndicated loans market.

C. Use of DLT in syndicated loans market

Having explained the main features of syndicated loans, below, I will explain the uses of DLT in the syndicated loans market. According to a survey dated November 2020, 17.7% of the members of the Loan Market Association are using or considering to use blockchain and smart contracts.[24] This is not surprising as DLT and smart contracts offer a lot of advantages for the financial services industry.

Before elaborating on the advantages of DLT for the actors of the syndicated loan market, one should explain the difference between a distributed ledger, blockchain and smart contracts.

I. Distributed ledger technology and smart contracts

DLT and smart-contracts would revolutionise the syndicated loans market, which is traditionally centralised and paper-based.

Distributed ledger is an innovative approach of recording, sharing and storing data in multiple registers.[25] Identical copies of such ledger is kept in several computers controlled by various users and this allows for simultaneous synchronisation of data.[26] Smart contracts, on the other hand, are computer programmes embedded in the blockchain and automatically performed by all nodes in the network. Due to their self-executing nature, smart contracts, automatically take action once the conditions written in the code are met. Combination of blockchain and smart contract technologies eliminates the need for intermediaries and speeds up the execution of transactions as written in the code.[27]

When used together, DLT and smart contracts offer a lot to the actors of the syndicated lending. Below, I will elaborate on the uses of such technology in the syndicated loans market.

---

[22]Fight (n 5) 8.

[23]Nirenberg (n 8) 161.

[24]Loan Market Association, 'LMA releases results of its members' survey: outlook for the syndicated loan market in 2021' <https://www.lma.eu.com/news-publications/press-releases?id=185> accessed 17 June 2023.

[25]Petrov (n 1) 88.

[26]Petrov (n 15) 9. Despite their close relationship, blockchain and distributed ledger are different concepts. Actually, blockchain is a type of distributed ledger. It refers to the technological data structure that stores and exchanges data packed in different blocks that are interconnected in a digital chain. It uses encryption and complex mathematical algorithms to provide irreversible and synchronized records. Petrov (n 1) 88.

[27]Petrov (n 15) 10.

II. What does DLT offer to the syndicated lending actors?

Interest in DLT is closely related to the existing factors that adversely affect the efficiency of the current and classical business model in the *primary* and *secondary market* of syndicated loans. In fact, distributed ledger technology and smart contracts are seen as significant tools to ease the negotiation, execution, administration and trading of loans in the syndicated loan markets. The most significant functions of DLT is that it eliminates the need for intermediaries; provides transparency, accuracy and authenticity; lowers transaction costs; makes it easier to comply with Know Your Customer obligations; and provides efficiency in the secondary market.

1. No need for intermediaries

In the financial services industry, institutional intermediaries play a significant role in the loan cycle starting from loan negotiations to settlement. They act as a bridge between the lenders and the borrower. They are responsible in keeping information on centralised databases with controlled access.[28] Intermediaries carry out the clearing and settlement concerning the loan. Settlement is made through the intermediaries and the average settlement times for syndicated loans are around 20 days.[29]

Smart contracts are self-executing in nature. The contract is automatically executed and such execution does not rely on the willingness or ability of the counterparty to fulfil his/her obligations. Therefore, smart contracts eliminate the risk of non-performance, minimise counterparty risk and eliminate the need to rely on third party intermediaries to follow through on commitments. As a result, using smart contracts to govern loan terms and conditions reduces manual labour and back-office workloads.[30]

Automation of certain processes makes the management of the syndicated loan process more efficient. In fact, a smart contract can be programmed to manage the whole process from negotiation to closing the deal without the need for human intervention.[31] For instance, DLT allows the investors to record their risk tolerance.[32] If a transparent and fully automated criteria is set, the syndicate can be formed by the smart contract easily, economically and swiftly.[33]

Smart contracts could also check parties' compliance with their contractual undertakings. For instance, in an automated way that is transparent to all parties, the smart contract could check whether one party complied with his financial covenants or delivered required documents.[34] Similarly, payment of the principal and interest, notice of unsettled debt and

---

[28]ibid. 9.

[29]M Buitenhek, 'Understanding and Applying Blockchain Technology in Banking: Evolution or Revolution?' [2016] Journal of Digital Banking 111, 117; Martino (n 4) 41.

[30]M Merike and A Steyn, 'Implementing Smart Contracts in the Syndicated Loan Market: An Issue of Adoption' [2019] IEEE Computer Society 39, 40.

[31]Petrov (n 15) 11.

[32]World Economic Forum, 'The Future of Financial İnfrastructure' (*World Economic Forum*, August 2016) 70 <https://www3.weforum.org/docs/WEF_The_future_of_financial_infrastructure.pdf> accessed 29 January 2023.

[33]Deloitte, 'Blockchain in Banking: While the Interest is Huge, Challenges Remain for Large Scale Adoption' (18 April 2017) 24 <https://www2.deloitte.com/content/dam/Deloitte/in/Documents/strategy/in-strategy-innovation-blockchain-in-banking-noexp.pdf> accessed 29 January 2023; D Petrov, 'Blockchain Technology – A Bank Lending (R)evolution: The Case of Syndicated Loans', New Challenges of Economic and Business Development – 2018: Productivity and Economic Growth: 10th International Scientific Conference 500, 504 <https://dspace.lu.lv/dspace/bitstream/handle/7/48890/Proceedings_NCEBD_2018.pdf?sequence=1#page=501> accessed 29 January 2023.

[34]K Fry-Paul, D Hirschfield and M Duric, 'Why are Smart Contracts the Smart Choice for Financial Services?' (22 February 2022) <https://www.taylorwessing.com/en/insights-and-events/insights/2022/02/why-are-smart-contracts-the-smart-

even use of collateral could be maintained automatically and without intervention of any intermediaries.[35] Since intermediaries are eliminated, settlement times could be shortened to hours or even minutes.[36] Shorter settlement times would reduce counterparty risks and increase liquidity in the market.[37]

2. Transparency, accuracy and authenticity

In the syndicated loan market, distribution of cash flows are tracked and managed manually in databases by a central trustee. Similarly, each lender reports data to a central database kept by a single recordkeeper in a central server.[38] As the loan documents are in PDF format and amendments are usually distributed by e-mail, this requires spending high amount of resources to reconcile such siloed information.[39]

DLT enables transaction records be kept in the computers of all participants as a whole and in real time. This increases the resilience and eliminates the need to rely on a single record keeping counterparty.[40] All authorised participants simultaneously have always-accurate records updated in real-time.[41] Parties could also access complete transaction chronology at all times. This is critical to prevent manipulation and falsification of data.[42] Immutable nature of the decentralised blockchain technology would practically decrease the data loss risk to zero.[43] Decreasing the amount of manual labour and automatising the transaction also decrease the risk of human-error.

Since all participants are informed about all transactions in real-time, this would ensure transparency.[44] Such transparency is also beneficial for the regulatory authorities for fulfilling their supervisory duties.[45]

As each participant uses his digital signature, each record on the ledger can be traced back to the concerned participant. As a result, authenticity of each transaction can be maintained.[46] Moreover, unlike the centralised banking system, which is susceptible to cyberattacks, blockchain is less prone to fraud as blockchain is immutable and every block has a timestamp.[47] Certainly, one should consider that the smart contracts are

---

choice-for-financial-services#:~:text=Smart%20contracts%20could%20be%20used,fall%20below%20a%20prescribed%20level> accessed 29 January 2023.

35 Petrov (n 33) 504; Deloitte, 'Over the Horizon: Blockchain and the Future of Financial Infrastructure' 10 <https://www2.deloitte.com/ch/en/pages/risk/articles/over-the-horizon-blockchain-and-the-future-of-financial-infrastructure.html> accessed 29 January 2023.

36 SA Rutenberg and RW Wenner, 'Blockchain Technology: A Syndicated Loan Revolution?' [2017] Financial Technology (FinTech) and Regulation, at 4; MH Sazu and S Akter Jahan, 'Impact of Blockchain-enabled Analytics as a Tool to Revolutionize the Banking İndustry' [2022] Data Science in Finance and Economics 275, 281.

37 G Padmanabhan and K Komma, 'Reinventing Syndicated Loan Processing with Distributed Ledger Technology' [2016] TCS Whitepaper; Buitenhek (n 29) 117.

38 Genpact, 'Impact of Distributed Ledger Technology on Syndicated Loans' 5 <https://www.genpact.com/downloadable-content/insight/impact-of-distributed-ledger-technology-on-syndicated-loans.pdf> accessed 29 January 2023.

39 M Casey and others, 'The Impact of Blockchain Technology on Finance: A Catalyst for Change' at 20 <https://www.sipotra.it/wp-content/uploads/2018/07/The-Impact-of-Blockchain-Technology-on-Finance-A-Catalyst-for-Change.pdf> accessed 29 January 2023.

40 D Shearer, 'Trade Finance and Distributed Ledger Technologies' [2018] Butterworths Journal of International Banking and Financial Law 99, 99.

41 Rutenberg and Wenner (n 36) 3.

42 Genpact (n 38) 6; Petrov (n 15) 9–10.

43 Petrov (n 15) 10.

44 U Ravindran and P Raghu Vamsi, 'A Secure Blockchain based Finance Application' IC3 '21: 2021 Thirteenth International Conference on Contemporary Computing (IC3-2021), August 2021 99, at 105.

45 Petrov (n 15) 11.

46 Petrov (n 33) 502.

47 Ravindran and Vamsi (n 44) 105; Sazu and Akter Jahan (n 36) 282.

only as good as they are drafted. In other words, a smart contract may be highly susceptible to attacks if they are not properly coded.

3. Lower transaction costs

The centralised nature and the paper-based operation of the syndicated loan market requires manual labour and back-office workloads throughout the whole cycle. It is estimated that transaction costs concerning syndicated loans would decrease around 70–80% through the application of the blockchain technology.[48] Certainly, this is an industry estimate and the actual decrease could be a lot less. However, one could expect a substantial decrease in such costs through automation of the syndicated loan process.

Blockchain technology simplifies and speeds up the completion of syndicated lending from about two weeks to one or two days.[49] Unlike the classical model, where intermediaries carry out the clearing and settlement concerning the loan, DL allows peer-to-peer interaction and smart contracts decrease settlement time and costs.[50] In fact, smart contracts would automatically check parties' compliance with their contractual undertakings and self-execute, which would reduce manual labour and back-office workloads.

4. Easier compliance with know your customer (KYC) obligations

KYC refers to an exchange of documents between the financial institutions and their customers to collect the customer's basic identity information.[51] Financial institutions are required to know the identity of their customers. This is critical to cope with money laundering and terrorism. Prior to opening a bank account, the customers are expected to fill long questionnaires and banks must verify such information. This is costly and time consuming. Moreover, such process is repeated each time a customer applies to a financial institution.[52]

DLT may be a useful asset in completing KYC activities in a faster and economical way. Selecting members of the syndicate requires a labour-intensive review of information pulled from multiple sources. The same applies for qualifying the borrower.[53] To solve this problem, a central KYC database could be created on the blockchain.[54] For instance, some scholars propose the following system to complete KYC over blockchain: Once a bank completes the KYC check for a new customer, information resulting from the KYC process could be uploaded to the blockchain. Such information could be accessed by other banks and accredited organisations (such as insurers, car rental firms, loan providers etc.). This would eliminate the need for the customer to re-start the KYC process all over again and reduce the administrative burdens and costs of the relevant institutions.[55] This would result in shorter waiting times and eliminate the need to provide the same information to different financial institutions.[56]

---

[48] Deloitte (n 33) 25.
[49] Noonan (n 3).
[50] Petrov (n 15) 9.
[51] Martino (n 4) 44.
[52] Sazu and Jahan (n 36) 280.
[53] Deloitte (n 36) 10.
[54] Rutenberg and Wenner (n 36) 4.
[55] Ravindran and Vamsi (n 44) 105; Martino (n 4) 45.
[56] Martino (n 4) 45.

There are other examples, which demonstrate that the use of technology could simplify KYC processes through their data sharing capabilities. For instance, open banking allows customers to provide their permission to securely share their financial information with approved third-party providers. As a result, financial institutions can instantly get essential information straight from the source and the customers are not required to produce same physical documents over and over again. Data standardisation and interoperability also enables easy information exchange between financial institutions, accelerating and simplifying KYC procedures. Similarly, the 'travel rule' also simplifies KYC processes to be conducted by financial institutions. As a set of guidelines by the Financial Action Task Force, the 'travel rule' requires financial institutions to communicate client information to each other in certain fund transfers. Although the travel rule primarily aims at preventing money laundering and terrorism financing, it also indirectly simplifies KYC procedures by enabling the effective exchange of KYC information in a standardised format.[57]

5. Efficiency in the secondary market

Smart contracts may provide efficiency in the trade of syndicated loans in the secondary market. For instance, if transfer certificates and assignment agreements are processed electronically, the smart contract could make the necessary checks under the facility agreement, execute the transfer of the loan, update the registry of the lenders and inform the borrower of the new lender.[58]

Tokenising the loans could also be beneficial. A token is a virtual representation of a reality such as an asset, right or duty within the context of a blockchain.[59] It is possible to issue electronic instruments on a DLT platform and these would represent entitlement to the receivable concerning the repayment of the loan. Such tokens could easily be traded and transferred on the platform. However, this raises the question if tokens would legally be deemed as transferrable securities.[60] Similarly, voting rights of the lenders may also be tokenised and whenever a decision needs to be taken among the lenders, voting tokens to be generated and distributed by the lead bank may be used.[61]

Despite all the advantages DLT offers for the syndicated loans market, there are important drawbacks that need to be addressed. In the next section, I will elaborate on such drawbacks and the need for proper regulation.

D. Drawbacks and the need for regulation

There are major drawbacks that prevent the utilisation of DLT in the syndicated loans market to the fullest extent. Some of these drawbacks can be overcome through technical means. However, there is need for the regulators' intervention and proper regulation to overcome some of these drawbacks.

---

[57]For differences between travel rule and KYC, see KYC-Chain, 'KYC Vs Travel Rule Compliance: What's the Difference?', <https://kyc-chain.com/kyc-vs-travel-rule-compliance-whats-the-difference/#:~:text=Put%20simply%2C%20KYC%20involves%20gathering,an%20FI%20or%20VASP%20facilitates> accessed 17 June 2023.

[58]Clifford Chance, 'The Digital Future of Syndicated Loans' (June 2021) 4 <https://www.cliffordchance.com/content/dam/cliffordchance/briefings/2021/06/the-digital-future-of-syndicated-loans.pdf> accessed 28 January 2023.

[59]On tokenization of the loan, see Gonzalez-Echenique (n 2) 326ff.

[60]Clifford Chance (n 58) 9.

[61]Gonzalez-Echenique (n 2) 327.

Firstly, it is questionable if it is practically possible to decentralise syndicated loans transactions entirely. It is apparent that blockchain to be used in syndicated loans market would be a permissioned or private blockchain rather than a public and permissionless one.[62] This is critical to maintain that only the authorised and concerned parties could access and make changes on the ledger. However, this would necessitate an element of centralisation as an operator would be needed to decide who will be permitted to the blockchain.[63] The more centralisation, on the other hand, means that the susceptibility to fraud and attacks would increase. Certainly, one could argue that such risk would still not be higher than the traditional syndicated loans transactions that are centralised and paper-based.

Secondly, conducting KYC over a shared ledger requires the financial institutions' agreement of a unified rating system[64] and the development of a common policy on the verification and identification of customers.[65] An interoperable system to transmit information between different financial institutions is also required.[66]

Thirdly, it is a matter of discussion if loans can be fully coded. Certainly, it would not be easy to automate a contractual clause, which is ambiguous or requires assessment. For instance, a material adverse effect clause that requires a reasonableness test. Although standardisation of loan documents could be helpful, it is not very easy to make as parties could prefer to negotiate the terms of their contract freely.[67]

It could be an option to partially automate syndicated loan process. For instance, many loan agreements have a clause that allows the lender to demand repayment of all outstanding loans in case of event of default by the debtor. Despite such provision, the lender may prefer not to exercise such right and negotiate with the borrower. It is apparent that a smart contract provision that automatically demands immediate repayment of outstanding loans would not be ideal at all times. Partial automation could be helpful in this regard: in an event of default, a smart contract could simply notify the lender that action is required, so that the lender would still have the opportunity to decide on accelerating the facilities or not.[68]

Fourthly, financial constraints would be highly effective in the actor's attitude towards blockchain technology, which is costly. Such cost is mainly associated with the energy consumption and storage space. Each blockchain transaction cost is approximately USD 0.20. Therefore, the technology could only spread if cost savings of the blockchain technology will outweigh the costs of such technology.[69]

Finally, financial services industry is a highly regulated market. Therefore, it might be expected that participation of the players in a distribution-ledger based market will also be subject to strict regulation and supervision. However, regulation is not only expected but also necessary. Because existing legal rules and institutions fail to create a predictable and legally safe environment for the spread of distributed ledger technology in the syndicated loans market. Among the several issues that require regulator intervention, the following are the most significant:

---

[62] Petrov (n 33) 508.
[63] Clifford Chance (n 58) 9.
[64] Petrov (n 1) 90.
[65] Sazu and Jahan, (n 36) 285.
[66] Martino (n 4) 46.
[67] Clifford Chance (n 58) 3–4.
[68] ibid 4.
[69] Sazu and Jahan (n 36) 285.

- Considering that blockchain is immutable, the legal system must clarify the status of the transactions on the blockchain if parties to a syndicated loan agreement are in dispute or litigation.[70] In a blockchain, data is recorded through a consensus mechanism and it is accepted that such mechanism guarantees the accuracy of the record. However, it is still unclear whether a court would consider such record to be legally accurate and admissible in case of a legal dispute.[71]
- Legal issues regarding the enforceability of smart contracts is another matter which needs to be addressed.[72] Especially, under many legal systems, security documents and inter-lender agreements that are usually executed as deeds cannot be created solely in smart contract format and signed by e-signatures.[73] Similarly, some legal systems may require some documents to be notarised and/or apostilled.[74] The same also applies to the transfer of the loans in the secondary market. For an effective use of DLT in syndicated loans market, legal order needs to be revised to grant validity to conducting relevant transactions as smart contracts and by using e-signatures.
- The existing legal framework must be revised to allow for an effective exercise of the supervisory functions of the regulatory authorities. If KYC activities are conducted through the distributed ledger, regulators may access and review all financial details in real-time and facilitate anti-money laundering and know your customer activities.[75] For instance, if the regulators have their own node on a distributed ledger, they could easily access information on the distributed ledger for regulatory purposes.[76] Due to the immutable nature of the blockchain, a comprehensible, secure and irreversible audit trail will be available to regulators. As regulators can independently access information on the DL, banks would no longer need to actively provide such data to prove their compliance.[77]
- Tokenising the loans would be functional, especially in trading the loans in the secondary market. However, it is disputed whether tokens could legally be deemed as transferrable securities, or not. If the legal order accepts token as a transferable security, in the secondary market, loans could be tokenised and such token could be traded and transferred on the platform.
- Although creating a central database may ease KYC obligations, compliance with data protection laws must be addressed to share the customer's personal data with other financial institutions.[78] In fact, such depository may also include personal data concerning the employees, e.g. the directors of the borrower.[79]
- Unprecedented legal disputes may arise. For instance, it might be necessary to decide who would be responsible if the code does not run as expected or data inputting is incorrect.[80] Proper ex-ante regulation could be valuable in eliminating or at least minimising such disputes.

---

[70]Petrov (n 1) 90.
[71]Genpact (n 38) 8.
[72]Stephen J Obie, 'Blockchain and the Syndicated Loan Market – a Closer Look' [2017] Butterworths Journal of International Banking and Financial Law 711, 712.
[73]Fry-Paul (n 34).
[74]Clifford Chance (n 58) at 6.
[75]World Economic Forum (n 32) 71.
[76]Casey and others (n 39) 22.
[77]Martino (n 4) 44.
[78]Martino (n 4) 45.
[79]Clifford Chance (n 58) at 8.
[80]ibid.

E. Conclusion

Syndicated loan market has a centralised nature, which is dominated by intermediaries. Transaction costs are high, manual labour and back-office workloads excessive and clearing and settlement times are long. DLT and smart contracts could be assets in overcoming these factors and ease the negotiation, execution, administration and trading of loans in the syndicated loan markets.[81]

Despite all that it offers, the existing legal rules and institutions fail to create a predictable and legally safe environment for the spread of distributed ledger technology in the syndicated loans market. Therefore, the primary requirement for widespread use of DLT technology in the syndicated loan market is proper regulation. However financial constraints would also be highly effective in the actor's attitude towards such technology.

One must keep in mind that DLT is not a technology that one bank can develop to win an advantage over its competitors. In fact, it could succeed if all participants work together.[82] Because widespread use and profitability of blockchain technology requires that the entire system adopts an interoperable system to transmit information.[83] However, one might expect that the existing financial intermediaries would resist such change to maintain their profitable position.[84]

Disclosure statement

No potential conflict of interest was reported by the author(s).

ORCID

Hüseyin Can Aksoy http://orcid.org/0000-0002-9243-189X

[81] Petrov (n 1) 90.
[82] Buitenhek (n 29) 119.
[83] Martino (n 4) 46.
[84] Petrov (n 1) 90.

The economic law of (central bank) digital currency

Filippo Zatti

ABSTRACT
The digital transformation of money has raised concerns about how it affects sovereignty. The rise of cryptocurrencies and the possibility of global payment systems based on stablecoins and digital currencies issued by central banks require a re-evaluation of the effects of these changes on the concept of money as a public good and legal tender. The analysis will start focusing on this experience and its implications to shift to the case where a cryptocurrency is used as a central bank currency. Then an attempt will be made to frame the distinctive features of a digital currency issued by a central bank.

A. Digital money as a (global) public good and (global) legal tender

Economists and legal scholars generally consider (fiat) money as a (global) public good, albeit specific.[1] However, such a statement is not so simple, and there is some disagreement.[2]

The definitions of 'public good' and 'money' can vary depending on the context, from economic and legal standpoints. We need to untangle this issue because if a currency is not a public good and the government has no reason to be the only provider of legal tender, the argument for a public monopoly in currency production becomes debatable. Technology's impact on the payments system and money supply means we must address this, even if it causes difficulties for regulators and rule-makers.

When it comes to economic law, searching for standards often requires assuming certain political principles to create effective regulatory models.[3] Therefore, it is crucial to carefully examine the underlying principles and values that inform these arguments to understand and fully evaluate their validity. The legal aspects are easier to understand than the economic ones. The reason could be the difficulty in discussing the concept of

[1]See Sarah Green, 'It is Virtually Money' in David Fox and Sarah Green (eds), *Cryptocurrencies in public and private law* (OUP 2019) 13 et seq.; Maria Rosa Lastra, 'Central Bank Digital Currencies (CBDCs) and the Case for Public Money' (*Centre for Commercial Law StudiesNews*, 7 April 2022) <https://www.qmul.ac.uk/ccls/news/2022/items/professor-rosa-lastra-delivered-the-4th-edinburgh-fintech-law-lecture.html>.
[2]See, forward, n 4 and n 6.
[3]See 'Box 1: Public versus private money, or a mix of both?' in Jean-Pierre Landau and Markus K Brunnermeier, 'The Digital Euro: Policy Implications and Perspectives' [2022] 53 Policy Department for Economic, Scientific and Quality of Life Policies Directorate-General for Internal Policies 12.

public good compared to money, especially when involving fiat currency.[4] It is due to the distinct forms that money today can take on and how it can be lawfully produced.[5] So, the discussion commonly focuses on what makes a currency universally acceptable instead of its production.[6]

The legal side has chosen 'fiat' as the solution, while economists lean towards the trust design model for creating money. Nowadays, considering the impact of technology on the payments system, the debate on the function of money seems pointless. Moreover, 'money production' appears to be confused with its issuance. The technological solution identified by Bitcoin's founder to create a bilateral payment system without an intermediary raises the question that money production can occur independently of politics and law. This 'item' can transfer without needing a trusted third party, unlike when it is produced by intermediaries, which instead rely on a reserved economic activity.[7]

The first is the case of cryptocurrencies. The incumbents showed a certain level of disregard towards them, perhaps due to their perceived similarity to the Ponzi scheme,[8] or even worse,[9] their classification as a security or commodity.[10] DLT-based currencies remind us that money is a social agreement that helps societies grow economically and socially in a market system.[11] This prompts us to re-evaluate the role of money as a resource for the public good. It is not just about keeping the financial system stable and prices in check or safeguarding people's savings. The credit and savings that come from achieving these goals can also be seen as public goods.[12]

---

[4]'The use of money is limited, as in the case of the park bench, and therefore, money is, according to the currently common scientific definition, an *'impure public good.'* However, there is an important aspect of money which constitutes a *'pure public good'*: money creates trust between people who do not know each other. The State establishes and supports the trust in *legal tender* and the official currency, making this trust a *'pure public good'* – non-excludable and non-rivalrous. The State puts various measures to create and maintain this trust: it issues money via the central bank; prescribes compulsory acceptance for legal tender; secures a portion of bank deposits; protects private property, and bails out banks:' see Christian Felber, *Money – The New Rules of the Game* (Springer 2017) 30. For a different conclusion about non-excludability and non-rivalry in money, see Lawrence White, *The Theory of Monetary Institutions* (Blackwell 1999) 89 et seq.

[5]For the concept, see at length Ann Pettifor, *The Production of Money: How to Break the Power of Bankers* (Verso 2017).

[6]On this point, see, for instance, the considerations proposed by White (n 4) 134-37.

[7]See Satoshi Nakamoto, 'Bitcoin: A Peer-to-Peer Electronic Cash System' 2 <https://bitcoin.org/bitcoin.pdf>.: 'In the mint-based model, the mint was aware of all transactions and decided which arrived first. To accomplish this without a *trusted party*, transactions must be publicly announced. We need a system for participants to agree on a single history of the order in which they were received.'

[8]See SEC – The Office of Investor Education and Advocacy, 'Ponzi Schemes Using Virtual Currencies' <https://www.sec.gov/files/ia_virtualcurrencies.pdf>.

[9]As stated by the Deputy Governor of the Reserve Bank of India: Shri T Rabi Sankar, 'Cryptocurrencies – An Assessment' (March 2022) Reserve Bank of India – RBI Bulletin 11, https://rbi.org.in/scripts/BS_ViewBulletin.aspx?Id=20870 quoting Robert McCauley, 'Why Bitcoin Is Worse than a Madoff-Style Ponzi Scheme' (*Financial Times*, 22 December 2021) https://www.ft.com/content/83a14261-598d-4601-87fc-5dde528b33d0.

[10]Jason G Allen, Henry Wells and Marco Mauer, 'Cryptoassets in Private Law: Emerging Trends and Open Questions from the First 10 Years' (2022) <https://www.ssrn.com/abstract=4206250>; Chiara Zilioli, 'Crypto-Assets: Legal Characterisation and Challenges under Private Law' (2020) <https://www.ssrn.com/abstract=3532316>; JG Allen, 'Property in Digital Coins' (2019) 8 European Property Law Journal 64, 69.

[11]For more on this concept, see the valuable contribution by Emilios Avgouleas and Sir William Blair, 'The Concept of Money in the 4th Industrial Revolution – A Legal and Economic Analysis' (2020) <https://www.ssrn.com/abstract=3534701>.

[12]See Michel Camdessus, 'International Financial and Monetary Stability: A Global Public Good' in Peter B Kenen and Alexander K Swoboda (eds), *Reforming the international monetary and financial system* (International Monetary Fund 2000) 10: 'When non-residents use national money, as is extensively the case for the world's major national monies, national monetary policies acquire aspects of *global public goods*. Exchange rates always, to some extent, involve issues of international public goods because an exchange rate is the relative price of two national monies and is affected by the corresponding national monetary policies. This international public goods aspect rises to global significance for exchange

Before deciding whether to allow privately created currency without intermediaries or regulate ventures like Bitcoin, it is crucial to consider the potential consequences concerning the values, principles, and financial goals of the relevant jurisdiction. Those three critical factors determine legal tender, and it is essential to carefully evaluate each element before deciding. When economic and legal systems are more closed, the differences in monetary systems may become more noticeable, but this may not always be true. On the other hand, when there is a greater exchange, the ontological differences on which design models are based may become less noticeable, but again, this may only sometimes hold. Moreover, while it is true that the idea of legal tender for money is rooted in the concept of sovereignty, other factors may contribute to the transition from considering money as a public good to accepting it as legal tender. Additionally, it is worth noting that the specific type of sovereignty that underlies legal tender can vary significantly across different jurisdictions, historically and currently, which could lead to significant differences in the implications and requirements of legal tender from one place to another.

When thinking about legal tender, it is essential to be cautious. Detailed analysis at the constitutional level shows that it is often connected to the ability to create and manage currency and safeguard credit and savings.[13] The digital transformation of money has raised concerns about how it affects sovereignty. Legal scholars have overlooked this topic, and this has led to confusion among economic scholars. However, the issue is now undeniable. The rise of alternative payment systems, such as cryptocurrencies, and the possibility of global payment systems based on stablecoins and digital currencies issued by central banks, require a re-evaluation of the effects of these changes on the concept of money as a public good and legal tender.

In light of this, examining how legal tender works in the case of cryptocurrencies and central bank digital currencies would be helpful. The recent decision by El Salvador to make bitcoin legal tender provides an opportunity to explore this topic further. In the next Section, the analysis will start focusing on this experience and its implications; the focus will then shift to the case where a cryptocurrency is used as a central bank currency and then, in Sections 4 and 5, an attempt will be made to frame the distinctive features of a digital currency issued by a central bank. To summarise, Section Six will provide additional insights on whether the digital transformation will impact the idea of legal tender, which was the initial topic of discussion.

B. The case for a 'forced legal tender'

El Salvador introduced bitcoin as a legal tender in a bill that entered into force on 7 September 2021.[14] The media and scientific sources report on the potential economic, legal,

rates among the world's major currencies because their use is global and movements in their exchange rates have widespread effects.'

[13] As in the case of art 47, Constitution of the Italian Republic. In the Italian legal system, the legal tender of the currency is mentioned in the civil code and is functional for fulfilling a contract. The Italian civil code at art 1277, in its book of obligations, provides that 'pecuniary debts are extinguished in the currency which is *legal tender* in the State at the time of payment and for its nominal value.'

[14] 'Ley Bitcoin', Decree No. 57, published in the Official Gazette No. 110, volume No. 430, 13 (June 9, 2021).

and political implications of adopting bitcoin as a 'forced' legal tender.[15] Both risks[16] and opportunities are being discussed and analysed.

Two critical issues need to be looked into further. The first is how El Salvador is connected to the IMF. [17] The second is the relationship between the Salvadoran government and its citizens about the new fiat money. El Salvador is trying to become financially independent.[18] The second issue involves the usage of bitcoin by Salvadoran citizens. The government cited financial inclusion[19] and the impact of remittances from immigrants to the US[20] as reasons for adopting bitcoin as legal tender. However, the decision has faced opposition from citizens[21], and the extent of usage remains unclear[22] despite the establishment of Chivo,[23] a government wallet loaded with $30 worth of bitcoin. The government has received permission to establish a $150 mln fund at the El Salvador State Development Bank (BANDESAL) [24] called 'FIDEBITCOIN'.[25] This fund's primary purpose is to ensure the seamless conversion of bitcoin to US dollars using Chivo and vice versa.[26] The 'Bitcoin law' is implemented based on some principles, technical standards and guidelines.[27] This complex regulatory framework is inevitable, as we are dealing

[15]As Steve Hanke, professor of applied economics at Johns Hopkins University, pointed out: see Shawn Tully, 'El Salvador's Plan to Create the First Bitcoin-Powered Nation Is Tanking the Economy – and Is a Mess by Every Measure' (*Fortune*, 20 January 2022) <https://fortune.com/2022/01/19/el-salvador-bitcoin-economy-distressed-debt/>.

[16]And how they can be addressed: see the El Salvador country team and IMF Western Hemisphere Department, 'El Salvador's Comeback Constrained by Increased Risks' (*IMF*, 16 February 2022) <https://www.imf.org/en/News/Articles/2022/02/15/cf-el-salvadors-comeback-constrained-by-increased-risks>.

[17]It is important to note that El Salvador renounced its national currency for the US dollar in 2000 and is experiencing growing indebtedness in a political context classified as illiberal. The Monetary Integration Act (El Salvador) 2020 [201]., which came into force on 1 January 2001, states in Art 3 that 'The dollar will have an unrestricted legal tender with the unlimited release for payment of obligations in money in the national territory.' Colón is still legal tender but not in circulation anymore. The fixed exchange rate was determined as follows: 1 $ for 8,75 ₡.

[18]As it is confirmed by its willingness to issue a bitcoin-denominated bond equal to a maturing bond valued in US dollars and with a high interest rate. Joshua Oliver and Tommy Stubbington, 'El Salvador Courts Crypto "Whales" as Traditional Investors Shun Bitcoin Bond' (*Financial Times*, 30 March 2022) <https://www.ft.com/content/4fa63c8c-51f5-4512-b522-76dd75e62916>.

[19]Banco Central de Reserva de El Salvador, 'Inclusión y educación financiera' (*Inclusión Financiera*) <http://inclusionfinanciera.gob.sv/>.

[20]'Topic: Bitcoin in El Salvador' (*Statista*, 7 September 2021) <https://www.statista.com/topics/8401/bitcoin-in-el-salvador/>; 'El Salvador Is Betting on Bitcoin to Rebrand the Country – and Strengthen the President's Grip' (*Time*,1 October 2021) <https://time.com/6103299/bitcoin-el-salvador-nayib-bukele/>.

[21]ibid.

[22]According to the 2022 first business survey of the Chamber of Commerce and Industry of El Salvador 'About the role of bitcoin as a legal tender and its impact on the performance of their businesses, 91.7% of the participants said that the implementation of bitcoin has been indifferent to their business, and 86% report that they have not made sales using cryptoassets. These percentages face only 3.6% of respondents claiming that bitcoin has contributed to increasing its sales, and 13.9% report having made sales in bitcoin.' See Chamber of Commerce and Industry of El Salvador, 'Businessmen Plan to Invest in El Salvador despite the Challenges Facing the Country' (10 March 2022) <https://camarasal.com/empresarios-proyectan-invertir-en-el-salvador-pese-a-los-retos-que-enfrenta-el-pais/>.

[23]Gobierno de El Salvador, 'Chivo Wallet' <https://chivowallet.com/chivowallet.com>.

[24]'Without prejudice to the actions of the private sector, the State will provide alternatives that allow users to carry out bitcoin transactions, as well as automatic and instant bitcoin-to-dollar convertibility if desired. The State will promote the necessary training and mechanisms for the population to access bitcoin transactions.'

[25]'Ley De Creación Del Fideicomiso Bitcoin', Decree No. 137, published in the Official Gazette No. 165, volume No. 432 (31 August 2021). See also BANDESAL, 'Reglamento Para El Funcionamiento Del Fidebitcoin' <https://www.bandesal.gob.sv/reglamento/>.

[26]Art 1 'Ley De Creación Del Fideicomiso Bitcoin' under the rules established by the Comité de Normas del Banco Central de Reserva de El Salvador, 'Normas Técnicas Para Facilitar La Aplicación de La Ley Bitcoin' <https://www.bcr.gob.sv/regulaciones/upload/Normas_Tecnicas_para_Facilitar_la_Aplicacion_de_la_Ley_Bitcoin.pdf>. As mandated by art 14, 'Prior to the entry into force of this law, the State shall guarantee, through the creation of a trust in the Banco de Desarrollo de El Salvador BANDESAL, the automatic and instantaneous convertibility of bitcoin to dollars of the alternatives provided by the State mentioned in article 8 of this law.'

[27]The 'Licensing Principles of Digital Wallet Platforms for Bitcoin and USD', the 'Technical Standards to Facilitate Bitcoin Law Enforcement' and the 'Technical Standards to Facilitate Financial Institutions' Participation in the Bitcoin

with a payment system rather than a currency based on a digital asset.[28] We are dealing with a decentralised and central payment system, as it requires the presence of an intermediary – Chivo, which BANDESAL represents through FIDEBITCOIN. However, this hybrid system loses some of the unique characteristics that Bitcoin's blockchain offers when it is not recognised as legal tender and can only be used as an alternative payment method or value circulation within a legal system. If the Salvadoran government objects to the regulations for virtual currencies, it could alter the nature of payment instruments. According to Article 7 of the FIDEBITCOIN operation regulations, operations must be confidential, as outlined by Salvadoran banking law, while still adhering to other laws such as BANDESAL Law, Bitcoin Law, and FIDEBITCOIN Law that regulate non-confidential information.

A question regarding El Salvador's current monetary policy needs to be addressed: What happens if the legal system recognises more than one currency as legal tender? While this is permissible by law, there may be economic and monetary implications. In an economic model where agents are involved, such as the current model, only one currency can be issued and managed by a central bank. The tax system is an expression of the State's financial policies. As a result, public finances and monetary sovereignty are closely linked.

C. The new digital form of money: lubricant or 'universal solvent' (alkahest)?

The monetary experiment in El Salvador demonstrates how blockchain technology and DLT can change the economic and legal framework of money.[29] However, it should be noted that this is only a theoretical perspective as there is no definitive empirical research data on the macro-drivers of cryptoassets.

Currently, cryptoassets are mainly not used to buy things, especially compared to other digital money types like bitcoin. Instead, cryptoassets are perceived as risk assets, potential macro hedges, and a tool to support cross-border payments.[30] One of the most important aspects of cryptoassets is their ability to facilitate transactions without the need for intermediaries. [31] Additionally, they are easy to store, transport, and access, which makes them a popular choice for people living in situations where they face threats from their families, communities, or governments.[32] When looking at real-world data on cryptoassets, there is evidence that goes against the norm when studying coins that are based on DLT but issued by governments directly or through central banks.

For example, the Marshall Islands (RMI) attempted to issue a cryptocurrency, but it was stopped before it could happen. In the case of RMI, there is a partial overlap with the Salvadoran legal framework, with the national currency being added as legal

Ecosystem' issued by the Central Bank of El Salvador, and the 'Guidelines for the Authorisation of the Operation of the Bitcoin and Dollar Services Technology Platform' published by the El Salvador Superintendency of the Financial System.

[28]This refers to a type of currency that is supported by a digital asset and is legally recognised as a financial instrument due to its unique features, including the use of a Blockchain with a specific algorithm.

[29]'El Salvador's Experiment with Bitcoin as Legal Tender' (*NBER*, July 2022) <https://www.nber.org/digest/202207/el-salvadors-experiment-bitcoin-legal-tender>.

[30]Erik HB Feyen, Yusaku Kawashima and Raunak Mittal, *Crypto-Assets Activity around the World: Evolution and Macro-Financial Drivers* (The World Bank 2022).

[31]Clemens Graf von Luckne, Carmen M Reinhart and Kenneth S Rogoff, 'Decrypting New Age International Capital Flows' <http://www.nber.org/papers/w29337>.

[32]'SEC.Gov | Paper, Plastic, Peer-to-Peer' <https://www.sec.gov/news/speech/peirce-paper-plastic-peer-to-peer-031521>.

tender to the US dollar, but it has no monetary authority. It may explain why the island Republic's Parliament approved an act on 'sovereign currency' (named 'SOV') to be issued as decentralised, based on blockchain technology,[33] through an Initial Currency Offering,[34] by the Ministry of Finance[35] in a sale of 24 million units.[36] However, SOV's features are mixed between those that are properly of a legal tender currency (for 'all debts, public charges, taxes, and dues'[37] and 'non-redeemable'[38] nature) and those that are instead of securities or financial instruments. It emerged by the involvement of the provisions of the Marshallese Banking Act and digital currency exchange regarding AML and the proxy to the Ministry of Finance to promulgate regulations to guarantee the monitoring of the ICO process and the SOV trading.[39] And even more, from the reserved destination to predefined fund trusts to serve national targeted needs,[40] also counting on the 40 per cent offering exclusively for non-Marshallese citizens. According to the Marshallese government's perspective, as explicitly stated in the SOV Foundation's whitepaper, SOV issuance was expected to serve a pure political economy provision other than monetary.[41]

The regulatory framework of the central bank and financial market needs an expensive administrative requirement for a small country to operate. The SOV whitepaper is particularly clear on this point. It emphasises how a monetary metre governed by blockchain technology – driven by an algorithmic protocol that sets its yearly growth at 4 per cent – allows for adopting a currency that is 'state' legal tender (in the economic sense of being linked to the national economy).[42] The IMF has repeatedly warned the tiny island republic of the risks involved in such a project. In particular, according to the IMF, SOV would challenge macroeconomic and financial stability and financial integrity.[43] Furthermore, SOV issuance could jeopardise the country's last US corresponding banking relationship with First Hawaiian Bank, exacerbating the access of RMI to global financial networks.[44] Whether one invokes the state theory of money[45] or the institutional approach, the functional view, or even the modern theory of money, we must not forget that 'issuing, managing, and sustainably maintaining a cryptoasset designated as legal tender is a complex endeavour and requires important prerequisites such as an adequate legal and regulatory

[33]Republic of the Marshall Islands, 'Declaration and Issuance of the Sovereign Currency Act 2018', Pub. L. No. 125ND2 P.L. 2018-53 (2018), para. 102, https://sov.foundation/law.pdf (Sovereign Currency Act).

[34]Sovereign Currency Act, para 104(4).

[35]Sovereign Currency Act, para 103(a).

[36]Sovereign Currency Act, para 105(2).

[37]Sovereign Currency Act, para 104(1).

[38]Sovereign Currency Act, para 104(5).

[39]Sovereign Currency Act, para 110(2).

[40]Budget and other national causes, mitigation of damages caused by global warming and climate change, protection of the fisheries and marine resources to ensure sustainable harvesting of tuna and other specials in the territorial waters, implementation of solar and other renewable energy facilities to reach 100 per cent sustainable energy resources, management and recycling of waste, investment into ecotourism projects, special needs of the people as a consequence of the US Nuclear Test Program, and distribution of SOV to Marshallese residents-citizens.

[41]SOV Foundation, 'The Marshallese Sovereign (SOV): Fair, Sustainable, Money' <https://perma.cc/XX2Y-MZ4X>.

[42]ibid 20.

[43]'IMF Executive Board Concludes 2021 Article IV Consultation with the Republic of the Marshall Islands' (*IMF*) <https://www.imf.org/en/News/Articles/2021/05/27/pr21142-marshall-islands-imf-executive-board-concludes-2021-article-iv-consultation>.

[44]Sonja Davidovic, 'The Marshall Islands SOV Deconstructed' (*The Global Fintech Intelligencer*, 8 June 2021) <https://theglobalfintechintelligencer.com/2021/06/08/the-marshall-islands-sov-deconstructed/>.

[45]See SOV whitepaper, Annex A.

framework, sufficient capacity to supervise and regulate the SOV, as well as the security of the underlying system, and a viable digital infrastructure.'[46] At the same time, however, we cannot dismiss what is clearly announced in the SOV whitepaper claiming international law: the legitimacy of exercising sovereignty as an independent nation issuing its own currency.[47]

Someone wonders if a 'central bank-less' decentralised monetary authority is acceptable to match the state or chartalist money theory as by Knapp. This theory requests the monopoly of legal tender. However, even if we could confirm that the coexistence of the US dollar and SOV would match the state theory of money conditions, we should consider one more aspect that, in the case of the Marshallese cryptoasset, remained unexperimented. Even if the duality of legal tender currencies could find an economic argument to justify it, the dimension of 'social technology' of money, i.e. its adoption beyond the formal legal level, should not be underestimated.

The Bahamas has taken a different step by introducing its own digital currency, the sand dollar, which follows standard monetary policy using blockchain technology. Although paper use is still more common than digital money, the government has set regulations encouraging the use of the sand dollar. The central bank has also integrated it with the Automated Clearing House system, opening up new possibilities for its use.[48] Around the same time the IMF published its Article IV Consultation, the Bahamas government released a policy white paper regarding the future of digital assets in the Bahamas. The para. 7 is concerned about the 'Bahamian's Access to Digital Assets'. It is a short paragraph, but it is pretty interesting – in the aims of this contribution – the following statement:

> We will work with the SCB, the Central Bank of The Bahamas, and the private sector on ways to enable Bahamians to access digital assets with B$, and for Bahamians to pay taxes using Sand Dollars. We will also seek to promote wider use of Sand Dollars in commerce on the islands.[49]

Even CBDCs remind us that of the three defining functions of money, only one is steadily in the hands of the government: a unit of account. The unit-of-account function remains the way to guarantee the nominal value of a currency for paying taxes and ensure its legal tender role.[50] CBDCs have all the characteristics to combine the three functions associated with money. It is essential to contemplate whether the surge of various payment instruments that serve as a store of value and medium of exchange could be a response to public control of money. If this is the case, what is the underlying reason for the emergence of such various payment options? It may be worthwhile to investigate the production methods and the rationale behind their creation thus far.

---

[46]Sonja Davidovic, 'The Marshall Islands SOV Deconstructed' (*Global Fintech Intelligencer*, 8 June 2021) <https://theglobalfintechintelligencer.com/2021/06/08/the-marshall-islands-sov-deconstructed>.

[47]SOV Foundation (n 41) 22.

[48]*The Bahamas: 2022 Article IV Consultation-Press Release; Staff Report; and Statement by the Executive Director for The Bahamas* (International Monetary Fund 2022) para 27 <https://www.imf.org/en/Publications/CR/Issues/2022/05/06/The-Bahamas-2022-Article-IV-Consultation-Press-Release-Staff-Report-and-Statement-by-the-517631>.

[49]'The Future of Digital Assets in The Bahamas – Office of the Prime Minister' (20 April 2022) <https://opm.gov.bs/the-future-of-digital-assets/>.

[50]Co-Pierre Georg and Katharina Pistor, 'The Right Response to the Libra Threat' (*Project Syndicate*, 5 August 2019) <perma.cc/3WJW-FJ4K>.

D. The 'taboo' of money

There is a significant shift in how money is legally classified. There are two primary design models for CBDCs: token-based and account-based. If the token-based model becomes the dominant choice, it would mean a renewed public money form with all three integrated functions.

How would this choice impact the banking sector and the institutional framework for monetary policy? Could the rise of digital currencies alter geopolitics and lead to a reform of the international monetary system? Would it ultimately spell the end of fiat currencies? Answering these questions is challenging due to their speculative nature and requires establishing an overall framework for the future monetary system. This involves determining if there is a legal model that can support economic systems that are independent of monetary policy.

The temptation could be to nationalise the creation of money that is in the power of the banks: 'banks would become only brokers of money they have on deposit, not creators of money, as is the case now.'[51] CBDCs may replace bank deposits but would not affect credit costs as the system can get funds from wholesale markets.[52] However, there is undoubtedly an impact on individual banks, if not in terms of operations, then certainly in the business model. The design model of CBDCs is linked to the lending function.

The first legal issue to be resolved could concern the notion of banking, at least as it is defined at the European level. It could also impact the universal bank model adopted in the EU banking system.

A second aspect concerns the governance of money. While the publicising of money creation facilitates the control of liquidity, it is also true that the evolutionary framework that the payments system may assume must be considered. In particular, the presence of digital currencies is also linked to fiat currencies issued by nonbanks. One regulatory aspect that has been partially resolved concerning the European system is asset-referenced tokens in the MiCAR. However, the stablecoin market still needs to be consolidated, and its shape will depend on the regulations proposed in other jurisdictions.

This picture must also add the impact that the choice of the CBDC design model will have on the monetary policy framework and the monetary authority itself. It is essential to exercise caution when considering border operations that rely on the convenience of holding nonspecific fiat currencies for one's country of residence. The potential consequences must be carefully assessed, including the impact on the currency's ability to govern in times of financial crisis, which could become less frequent but more severe. Additionally, the role of the digital dollar in the international monetary system may be diminished by the emergence of other digital currencies, such as the digital euro and the digital yuan. These factors must be considered before making any decisions regarding border operations and currency holdings.[53]

---

51 Daniel Pinchbeck and Ken Jordan, *What Comes After Money?: Essays from Reality Sandwich on Transforming Currency & Community* (Evolver Editions 2011) 127.

52 Toni M Whited, Yufeng Wu and Kairong Xiao, 'Central Bank Digital Currency and Banks' (2022) <https://www.ssrn.com/abstract=4112644>.

53 'Digital Currencies: The US, China, And The World At A Crossroads' (Hoover Institution Press 2022) 55 ff. <https://www.hoover.org/research/digital-currencies-us-china-and-world-crossroads>.

E. The legal dimension of digital money issued (or not issued) by a central bank

While there has been extensive analysis of the topic from an economic perspective, there needs to be more legal studies on the issue.[54] One of the first papers concerning the legal aspect of CBDC from an international perspective was published by a group of researchers at the Legal Department of the IMF in 2020[55] and focused their legal analysis on two main issues. First, it concerns verifying the suitability of the central bank's mandate to issue a digital currency and its qualification as a legal tender; the other concerns monetary law, meaning the currency system.

The first is a critical legal question associated with the issuance of CBDCs and regards the extension of the legal framework of legal tender to digital currency. The other is the idea of adopting a standalone regime for CBDCs. These are critical aspects in defining the status of a CBDC, whether it is the digital version of the physical currency, which is legal tender, or whether it is a different currency pegged by the mere fact of being central bank money.

However, it might be helpful to take a step back and examine a distinct point about the current situation – namely, the infrastructure on which the monetary system is built. If a digital currency is issued thanks to a DLT, as appears to be the most plausible solution to date, or to a Blockchain, that currency is, first and foremost, a token based on that infrastructure. It could be argued that this is a neutral technological choice, changing the instrument that makes the currency circulate, not its legally codified nature. One crucial point that many legislators seem to overlook is the role of dematerialisation in fiat monetary systems. The current physical system helps to facilitate the exchange of money, which is crucial for the global economy. However, it is important to note that the materials used for banknotes and coins are irrelevant from a private law perspective. These physical objects are just material superstructures that take on the character of fiat under legal acts. The law itself is the infrastructure that governs the system.

Regarding DLT or Blockchain infrastructure, these systems have their own rules, which do not necessarily need to be defined by the law. Even if they were, they could escape legal confines. The rise of cryptocurrencies in 2009 and stablecoins in the last decade has shown that central bank infrastructures are no longer the only option available. Overall, it is essential to consider the impact of technological advancements on monetary systems and recognise that the system's infrastructure is not solely determined by physical materials but by legal acts and technological developments.

Scholars and central bankers are still debating the concept of 'Moneyness'. However, fiat currency's lack of intrinsic value becomes more complicated when analysing digital currencies on DLT. A vital inquiry arises regarding the legal tender status of currency and its relation to its physical or digital form. Should the response be harmful, the legal implications extend beyond determining currency's validity as a legal tender. In such a case, legal tender status would be granted only to fiat money issued by a central bank,

---

[54]See for more details Toni Ahnert and others, *The Economics of Central Bank Digital Currency* (European Central Bank 2022); Ratikant Bhaskar and others, 'Central Bank Digital Currencies: Agendas for Future Research' (2022) 62 Research in International Business and Finance 101737.

[55]Wouter Bossu and others, 'Legal Aspects of Central Bank Digital Currency: Central Bank and Monetary Law Considerations' (2020) 20 IMF <https://www.imf.org/en/Publications/WP/Issues/2020/11/20/Legal-Aspects-of-Central-Bank-Digital-Currency-Central-Bank-and-Monetary-Law-Considerations-49827>.

despite possessing only one technical characteristic in common with physical currency. All other technical features would render it akin to a form of cryptocurrency, albeit with particularly notable distinctions. To clarify, we would not be dealing with a single coin issued on one particular blockchain. However, we would still encounter legal issues affecting digital currencies instead of physical money. This is especially apparent when dealing with a wholesale CBDC, as it operates similarly to current settlement systems like RTGS. The situation is different for a retail CBDC or a stablecoin, which are forms of digital money designed for the public. The question arises whether they are various forms of public money or not.

An excellent example of focusing better on the point is what happens to the banknotes in Scotland. Commercial banks issue the Scottish pound, but the Bank of England fully backs it. However, in the case of the Scottish digital pound, it would differ from now. Therefore, the border between public and private money varies in the case of its digital representation on DLT-based tokens. The fact is that DLT and blockchain technology allow going beyond the dematerialisation of money (as in the case of e-money) towards its desovereignisation. A fence that, at least in Europe, has its roots in the 'first contact' between sovereign and bankers' money dating back to the sixteenth century.[56] And that is now challenged by the specificities of DLT, which can guarantee the creation of relatively resilient networks concerning the enforcement capacity at the jurisdictional level.

DLT and Blockchains tend to eliminate central control, which can shift the balance between public and private money towards the latter. This has a range of structural effects. The development of stablecoins can be traced back to various reasons beyond financial inclusion. Stablecoins serve as a link between traditional finance and decentralised finance. Due to their pseudo-crypto nature, they are attractive to those seeking a disintermediated payment system. However, the history of Libra/Diem and the Terra-Luna crash shows that maintaining stability in a currency, even with fiat collateral in a centralised monetary system, can be complex and produce systemic effects. Monetary contexts prioritise protecting constitutional interests rather than just monetary objectives, which can be challenging to balance. Despite uneven balancing across legal systems, the Bretton Woods agreements provide a monetary system framework. Economic law shows that digital currencies have a private law dimension, which reflects their ability to either evade or comply with regulatory authority control. The impact of a future CBDC introduction on public money as legal tender is a crucial question. It remains to be seen whether the legal system will need to adapt to facilitate digital currency issuance. However, the implications of this issue extend far beyond mere theoretical or nominalistic significance.

F. Would digital reshaping of money affect legal tender? Some final considerations

Legal tender has traditionally been associated with cash since the introduction of fiat currency. However, it is now commonly accepted that deposits should also be considered

[56] Marie-Thérèse Boyer-Xambeu, Ghislain Deleplace and Lucien Gillard, *Private Money & Public Currencies: The 16th Century Challenge* (ME Sharpe 1994).

legal tender. This is an essential consideration for any digital solutions aimed at the general public.

Money serves as a public good by ensuring secure economic transactions through its role as a unit of account in financial and legal matters. Legal tender currency, in the form of paper money from central banks and private money from commercial banks, guarantees the value of transfers and is recognised as part of the legal system. With the rise of electronic payment systems, monetary obligations are now being fulfilled through account settlements without exchanging physical currency.[57] Therefore, the additional innovation allowed by DLT-based means of payment will gradually replace cash and, perhaps, the way we currently mean deposits. We would have 'two different popes' with distinct legal features for a defined period[58], which means both as a currency in itself (see privacy over everything) and in terms of the impact it will have on the banking and monetary systems.

On the other hand, today, cash is intermediated through the banking system to various payment systems. Once a CBDC is issued, whichever model is chosen by the monetary authority, we will inevitably face greater ease of circulation of currencies with a different national sphere of influence than at present. The necessary interrelation of payment systems will facilitate the competition between payment means in digital legal tender coins issued by central banks and the role of stablecoins likely played alongside legal tender coins.[59]

Many issues that today find an answer in commonly accepted practises of the central banks (at least at the BIS level) are put under review since it is becoming more and more concrete the possibility that CBDCs would become a reality. Based on the limited use cases analysed earlier, the experience suggests a primary point of consideration. Although CBDCs may be recognised as legal tender, consumers are likely to use them infrequently due to concerns about privacy and surveillance. As a result, cash would remain the preferred option. Let's revisit where we began. Money is unlike any other public good, and user confidence is crucial for public money to succeed. To promote the marketability of CBDC, it is essential to encourage confidence. The main issue is not only market factors – building a network of merchants that accept and encourage CBDC use, achieving interoperability with and enlisting participation from the traditional banking sector – but the recasting of the role of public powers in effectively controlling the liquidity and soundness of the 'national' financial system. It is no coincidence that the debate on the issuance of CBDC has been confronted in each exploring country with the need to amend the rules on the power to issue money as legal tender.[60] The introduction of a

[57]Kazuaki Sono, 'Legal Tender: A Notion Associated with Payment' in IMF, *Current Developments in Monetary and Financial Law, Vol. 2* (International Monetary Fund 2003) 679 ff. <https://elibrary.imf.org/openurl?genre=book&isbn=9781589061767>. On this specific point, see also Vincenzo De Stasio, 'Verso Un Concetto Europeo Di Moneta Legale: Valute Virtuali, Monete Complementari e Regole Di Adempimento' (2018) 6 Banca, Borsa e Titoli di credito 749 ff.

[58]Aminu Adamu Ahmed, Alhaji Adamu Saidu and Jibril Hussein Kawure, 'The Roles of Central Bank Digital Currency over Physical Currency' (2022) 1 International Journal of Social Science, Education, Communication and Economics 75.

[59]This is especially so if a decentralised financial ecosystem (DeFi) is developed. Moreover, what is happening in the payment system is emblematic of the changing needs and objectives of economic policy in the EU. The announcement of a European sovereign wealth fund can no longer be read in terms of cooperative regulation or regulatory competition. Still, a single public policy and policy design sounded on resilience. It is to wonder if monetary policy would be neutral in the long term.

[60]In the Euro Area, a draft on digital euro legal tender was released in June 2023.

digital currency that is recognised as legal tender does not solely confine legal experts to the study of its privacy features, its correlation with conventional legal tender, and the aspects commonly examined in monetary law. As we delve deeper into this topic, we must recognise that additional factors and ramifications could be considered. This study naturally expands into public and international law realms, where various inter-twined issues arise in connection with the progressive 'desovereignisation' we previously discussed. With the introduction of CBDC, it will be possible to make legal tender-based cross-border payments, allowing for easier maintenance of funds in the incoming foreign currency.[61] One potential strategy to consider would be to set limits on the use of digital legal tender through a cap or statutory restrictions. This approach could prove effective, particularly in cases where legal tender is intended for specific purposes, such as public assistance projects or poverty relief. By taking this step, it may be possible to better manage the use of digital legal tender and ensure that it is being utilised responsibly and appropriately. The limited impact on monetary policy would classify it as an alternative payment instrument. Let us examine the highly developed CBDC initiative of e-CYN in economically advanced nations. It is worth noting that a civil code provision took effect in 2021, in addition to the proposed amendment to the law on the People's Bank of China to grant recognition of legal tender to the e-CYN. It states that 'where an obligation is a payment of money unless otherwise provided by law or agreed by the parties, the creditor may ask the debtor to perform in the legal tender of the place of actual performance.'[62] This rule could potentially clash with monetary sovereignty, especially regarding the renminbi and its digital version. It adds nothing more than acknowledging that a legal digital currency also influences aspects of solvency law. The significance of preserving the legal value of money in modern times is to ensure the operation of a multilevel monetary payment system dominated by the 'national' currency.

However, that provision does not appear comparable to the '*datio in solutum*' because it explicitly concerns cross-border transactions. To guarantee the '*best choice status*' of the 'national' or official currency or the '*finality*' of the debt settlement,[63] the government can use market instruments to improve its own currency management in an environment that allows competition from other currencies, or it can use mandatory legal tools to make the national currency legally solvent. Significant in this regard is what is stated in Art. 65 of the People's Bank of China Law concerning the issuance of digital tokens produced or offered for sale for circulation in the market instead of the *digital renminbi*. The Chinese central bank can order the illegal act to cease, destroy the illegally created and distributed digital tokens, confiscate the illegal income, and impose a fine.[64] Here, the legal tender is therefore interpreted as a function of a modern payment system but does not go so

[61] FinTech Department, 'Concept Note on Central Bank Digital Currency' 14 <https://rbidocs.rbi.org.in/rdocs/PublicationReport/Pdfs/CONCEPTNOTEACB531172E0B4DFC9A6E506C2C24FFB6.PDF>.

[62] Civil Code of the People's Republic of China 2020, art 514.

[63] On this specific point see Rosa Giovanni Barresi 'La Convivencia Entre Digital Euro Y Digital Asset' in Filippo Zatti and Rosa Giovanna Barresi, 'La futura gobernanza del sistema monetario internacional: primeras consideraciones sobre el papel del euro digital' in Carmen Pastor Sempere (ed), *Dinero digital y gobernanza TIC en la UE* (Editorial Aranzadi 2022).

[64] It is at most five times the illegal amount; if it cannot be determined, a fine of not less than 100,000 yuan but not exceeding 500,000 yuan shall be imposed. If the circumstances are severe, a penalty shall be imposed under art 61 (2) of the Law on the People's Bank of China. See Law of the People's Republic of China on the People's Bank of China (Draft for Comments on the Revised Draft) State Council of the PRC, '中国人民银行关于《中华人民共和国中国人民银行法(修订草案征求意见稿)》公开征求意见的通知_银行_中国政府网' (23 October 2020) <http://www.gov.cn/zhengce/zhengceku/2020-10/24/content_5553847.htm>.

far as to recognise the possible issuance of tokens linked to legal tender. By contrast, the US and UK had hitherto considered the issuance of CBDCs as not strictly necessary, grasping its libertarian implications but underestimating the aspect of monetary sovereignty.[65] It has led the EU countries to consider the issuance of a digital euro for the reasons at the basis of MiCAR. In the context of transnational organisations like the G7, the G20, or the IMF, these reasons can only be partially considered.[66] Legal scholars and policymakers need to pay attention to the potential risks posed by CBDCs. These digital currencies can potentially affect the international monetary system, and it is vital to ensure that appropriate and coherent reforms are put in place. This is especially urgent now that the concept of legal tender is being discussed concerning digital currencies.[67]

Disclosure statement

No potential conflict of interest was reported by the author(s).

ORCID

Filippo Zatti http://orcid.org/0000-0002-1528-3045

[65]'See the Speech by Vice Chair for Supervision Quarles on Central Bank Digital Currency' (Board of Governors of the Federal Reserve System) <https://www.federalreserve.gov/newsevents/speech/quarles20210628a.htm>.

[66]G7 United Kingdom, 'Public Policy Principles for Retail Central Bank Digital Currencies (CBDCs)' <https://assets.publishing.service.gov.uk/government/uploads/system/uploads/attachment_data/file/1025235/G7_Public_Policy_Principles_for_Retail_CBDC_FINAL.pdf>; FSB, 'G20 Roadmap for Enhancing Cross-Border Payments: Consolidated Progress Report for 2022' (2022) <https://www.fsb.org/wp-content/uploads/P101022-1.pdf>; *Options for Access to and Interoperability of CBDCs for Cross-Border Payments (Report to the G20)* (BIS 2022) <https://www.bis.org/publ/othp38.pdf>; Chusu He, Alistair Milne and Markos Zachariadis, 'Central Bank Digital Currencies and International Payments' (17 May 2022) <https://papers.ssrn.com/abstract=4112382>.

[67]See namely Filippo Zatti, 'Nuevas Oportunidades Y Desafíos De La Emisión De Digital Asset Por El Banco Central Para La Gobernanza Del Sistema Monetario Internacional' in Zatti and Barresi (n 63).

Regulating virtual asset service providers in the offshore world: the Cayman Islands example

Andrew James Perkins

ABSTRACT

This article will seek to firstly, outline the reasons why virtual asset service providers have embraced trading offshore. Secondly, it will evaluate the Cayman Islands legislative regime under the Virtual Asset Service Providers Act and its associated regulations to test compliance with international regulatory standards. Thirdly, it will consider the international focus that the Cayman Islands attracts on issues of global taxation and the prevention of money laundering, and will evaluate how Cayman has approached the new challenges presented by cryptocurrencies whilst demonstrating compliance with international standards. This article will reach conclusions as to how offshore regulators and their legal frameworks are going to need to adapt and keep pace with the evolution of cryptocurrencies so that they can protect the integrity of their valuable financial services industries. Offshore jurisdictions should not be seen as selling the crypto industry the shovels with which to mine, if that would involve undermining compliance with regulatory, anti-money laundering and tax transparency standards.

A. Introduction

The origins of distributed ledger technology can be traced to the aftermath of the financial crash of 2007–2009. The goal was to establish private virtual currencies that did not rely on the issuing of a central bank as a third party, instead replying upon the integrity of its miners to establish trust.[1] Today over 9000[2] different crypto assets exist, allowing for a digital representation of value that can be digitally traded, transferred, or used for payments. The distributed ledger technology allowing cryptocurrencies, such as bitcoin, to function creates a perpetually continuous list known as blockchain which records individual transactions between users. Every time a user sells or transfers a unit of the virtual currency, the blockchain records the transaction and acts like a bank ledger.[3] Within the blockchain however, unlike at a bank, very little know your customer (KYC) information is recorded about the identity or

[1] S Nakamoto, 'Bitcoin: A Peer-to-Peer Electronic Cash System' <https:/bitcoin.org/bitcoin.pdf>.

[2] <https://coinmarketcap.com/> (visited 23 February 2023).

[3] Blockchain – The Next Big Thing (*The Economist*, 9 May 2015) <https://www.economist.com/news/special-report/21650295-or-it-next-big-thing>.

location of the user. The blockchain only records a hashed code containing a string of numbers and letters.[4] Unsurprisingly, this has resulted in trading in virtual assets being attractive to criminals, particularly with laundering proceeds of crime on the blockchain. Moreover, the use of obfuscating technology has further enabled criminals to conceal the transaction path and provide enhanced anonymity.[5] Virtual assets have been used on the dark web for the purchase of drugs, weapons, to procure child pornography[6] as well as for traditional money laundering activities. It has been estimated that these activities account for up to 46.17% of all bitcoin transactions.[7]

The challenge of building a regulatory structure for virtual assets and its associated technology is, however, complex and uncertain. Regulators must balance the exploding popularity of virtual assets against several complicated factors. Firstly, the anonymous nature of the technology. Secondly, their potential to undermine the stability of the global economy[8] through use in money laundering and tax evading activities. Thirdly, governments need to balance the revenue that can be generated from virtual asset transactions against the enactment of market security measures to ensure the virtual asset market is adequately policed and that transactions are secure.

Offshore jurisdictions such as the Cayman Islands have implemented regulatory structures to support the growth of virtual assets and to encourage financial institutions to invest in them.[9] As a tax neutral hub, Cayman is one of the world's top financial jurisdictions and the go-to destination for the formation of investment funds. In fact, 49% of crypto hedge funds and 42% of crypto fund managers are domiciled in the jurisdiction.[10] The Cayman Islands government have expanded their ambitions beyond just being a financial hub but also seek to become a global technology hub.[11] Cayman has established a Special Economic Zone to provide virtual asset businesses with a simplified route to gaining a physical presence within the Jurisdiction. The virtual asset industry is also subjected to a regulatory framework centred around the Virtual Asset Service Providers Act. This regime attempts to implement the recommendations of the Financial Action Task Force (FATF) on international standards for combating money laundering and the financing of terrorism and proliferation, as applicable to virtual assets and their service providers.

This article will seek to firstly, establish why virtual asset service providers (VASPs) have embraced trading offshore. Secondly, it will evaluate the Virtual Asset Service Providers Act to test compliance with international best practice. Thirdly, considering the regular international focus on the issues of global taxation and the prevention of money

[4]S Mbiyavanga, 'Cyrptolaundering: Anti Money Laundering Regulation of Virtual Currency Exchanges' (2023) 3(1) Journal of Anti-Corruption Law 1–15.

[5]R Barone and D Masciandaro, 'Cryptocurrency or Usury? Crime and Alternative Money Laundering Techniques' (2019) 47 European Journal of Law and Economics 223–54.

[6]U.S. Department Of Justice 'Report Of the Attorney General's Cyber Digital Task Force: Cryptocurrency enforcement framework' (2020) <https://www.jusice.gov/cryptoreport>.

[7]S Foley, JR Karlsen, and TJ Putnins, 'Sex, Drugs and Bitcoin: How much Illegal Activity Is Financed Through Cryptocurrencies?' (2019) 32(5) The Review of Financial Studies 1798–835.

[8]C Albrect and others, 'The Use of Cryptocurrencies in the Money Laundering Process' (2019) 22(2) Journal Of Money Laundering Control 210–16.

[9]B Molloy, 'Taxing the Blockchain. How Cryptocurrencies Thwart International Tax Policy' (2019) 20 Oregon Review of International Law 643–47.

[10]PWC, '4th Annual Crypto Hedge Fund Report' (2022) <https://www.pwc.com/gx/en/financial-services/pdf/4th-annual-global-crypto-hedge-fund-report-june-2022.pdf>.

[11]Technology City Cayman Islands | Cayman Enterprise City < https://www.caymanenterprisecity.com/cayman–tech>.

laundering, evaluate how the Cayman Islands have approached the new challenges presented by cryptocurrencies whilst attempting to comply with stringent international compliance standards. This article will seek to demonstrate that offshore regulators and their legal frameworks are going to need to continually adapt to keep pace with the evolution of virtual assets so that a level of protection can be offered to the integrity of their valuable financial services industries.

B. Context: why should states regulate virtual assets?

Regulation of virtual assets and those that provide services in relation to them are one of the key financial policy issues of our day. The challenges of regulation are immense as the technology, business practices and uses of virtual assets vary significantly from traditional financial services.[12] Furthermore, the rapid speed of innovation and complexity of the technology can make traditional regulatory strategies difficult to apply. Various methods of regulation have become standard practice in financial markets and include principles-based regulation, outcome focused regulation, management regulation, risk-based regulation, judgment-based regulation and credible deterrence.[13] The lack of a central entity or traditional intermediary to be subjected to a regulatory authority is a unique challenge in the virtual asset space. This is further enhanced, when users of virtual assets would be partial to a low regulatory ceiling[14] and classically financial regulators err on the side of caution when applying standards.

The regulation of virtual assets has caused all sorts of headaches for policy makers, regulators and the courts. Virtual assets do not fit easily into any defined category of financial products already in existence. The regulatory community has had to grasp whether virtual assets are money because they store value as a unit of account, or whether virtual assets are an investment product because they are used to generate wealth in the future. Through virtual assets uses, regulators have also had to grapple with the fact that virtual assets have become an encompassing and society wide system for keeping up with who owns what[15] with a value as real as money in a bank.[16] Regulators have however, also been confronted with estimates that virtual asset transactions account for between 3% and 4% of all laundered proceeds worldwide,[17] a concerning statistic, leading to stark warnings from regulators about the use of virtual assets.[18] Reasons for these warnings stem from the fact that virtual

---

[12]B Hemenway and S Hammer 'A Comprehensive Approach to Crypto Regulation' (2023) 25 University of Pennsylvania Journal of Business Law, 415.

[13]For reviews of types of regulation see R Baldwin, M Cave and M Lodge (eds), *Oxford Handbook On Regulation* (OUP 2012).

[14]M Field, 'Bitcoin Companies For First UK Body As Regulators Circle' (*Telegraph*, 13 February 2018).

[15]MJ Casey and P Vigna, 'Bitcoin and the Digital Currency Revolution' (*The Wall Street Journal*, 23 January 2015) <http://www.wsj.com/articles/the-revolutionary-power-of-digital-currency-1422035061>.

[16]D Keopsell, 'Rise of the Cryptocurrencies Like Bitcoin Begs Question: What is Money?' *(The Conversation*, 25 September 2015) <https://theconversation.com/rise-of-cryptocurrencies-like-bitcoin-begs-question-what-is-money-46713>.

[17]R Wainwright, 'Crypto Money-Laundering Will Crypto Help the Money Launderers of the Future?' (*The Economist*, 26 April 2018) <https://www.economist.com/finance-and-economics-2018/04/26/crypto-money-laundering>.

[18]FATF, 'Virtual Assets, Red Flag Indicators of Money Laundering and Terrorist Financing' (September 2020), FATF 'Updated Guidance for a Risk Based Approach to Virtual Assets and Virtual Asset Service Providers' (October 2021) and FATF 'Virtual Assets: Targeted Update of the FATF Standards on Virtual Assets and Virtual Asset Service Providers' (June 2023).

asset products have turned out to be scams,[19] and found to contain misleading investment information.[20] In some cases virtual asset products have also been sensitive to hacking.[21] A lack of safeguards in place to protect consumers have also caused concern for regulators and if a financial crisis was to take hold in the virtual asset sphere there would be limited recourse as virtual assets by their nature are generally not backed by a central bank or government.[22] Tax evasion has also caused concern with the use of virtual assets being seen as a means of avoiding paying national taxation.

However, whilst balancing these negatives regulators have had to recognise that virtual asset transactions can bring distinct advantages to those conducting cross border transactions. They allow for a cheaper and faster way in which to conduct commercial transactions.[23] Virtual asset use can also act as an alternative form of capital market financing through the process of peer-to-peer lending. Virtual assets also bring an access advantage meaning that they can be accessed by the general population who may not have access to other systems of finance.[24] Taking these considerations onboard, national supervising authorities have frequently pondered with how to enact legislation to regulate the virtual asset arena. Generally, states have enacted a legislative package consisting of three main features namely financial markets legislation, including that of securities, anti-money laundering (AML) legislation and consumer law.[25] However, legislative structures surrounding intricate virtual asset technology are piecemeal and fragmented ranging from a negative approach obstructing trade through to a positive and facilitating approach.

Jurisdictions including Bangladesh and Qatar have banned the use of cryptocurrencies justifying the need for such stringent control by reference to the use of volatile virtual assets in the money laundering process and its associated crimes. In China, Iran, and Turkey cryptocurrency cannot be used as financial assets in banks or be traded or used for domestic payments. Elsewhere cryptocurrency is used though with a sense of suspicion. In the United Kingdom, the Financial Conduct Authority has introduced a cooling off period for first time investors, banned refer a friend bonuses and put rules in place to ensure that advertising is not misleading.[26] In contrast, in El Salvador bitcoin now has the status of legal tender, with half of the nation's households downloading a government sponsored app in order to promote and normalise its use.[27] In the Cayman Islands, the real estate industry has just celebrated very publicly in the media its first property sale

---

[19]The Australian Government the Treasury. Initial Coin Offerings. Issues Paper. The Commonwealth of Australia: TSY/AU [2019]. https://static.treasury.gov.au/uploads/sites/1/2019/02/c2019-t353604-Issues_Paper.pdf, p. 7; see: /https://www.fsma.be/en/warnings/cryptocurrency-fraud-dont-be-taken.

[20]ESAs warn consumers of risks in buying virtual currencies (europa.eu) https://www.esma.europa.eu/press-news/esma-news/esas-warn-consumers-risks-in-buying-virtual-currencies.

[21]J Simser, 'Bitcoin and Modern Alchemy: In Code We Trust' (2015) 22(2) Journal of Financial Crime 156–69.

[22]TA Anderson, 'Bitcoin – It is Just a Fad? History, Current Status and the Future of the Cyber-Currency Revolution' (2014) 29 Journal of International Banking Law and Regulation 428–35.

[23]JJ Oerlemans and others, 'Cybercrime en witwassen: bitcoins, online dienstverleners en andere witwasmethoden bij banking malware en ransomware.Onderzoek en beleid WODC' (2016) (319) Meppel: Boom Criminologie 62.

[24]C Chambers-Jones, 'The Financial Crisis and Digital Currencies' in M Ryder (ed), *White Collar Crime and Risk. Palgrave Studies in Risk, Crime and Society* (Palgrave Macmillan 2018) 203–30.

[25]B Custers and L Overwater 'Regulating Initial Coin Offerings and Cryptocurrencies: A Comparison of Different Approaches in Nine Jurisdictions Worldwide' (2019) 10(3) European Journal of Law and Technology 29.

[26]Financial Conduct Authority, 'Financial Promotion Rules For Crypto Assets', PS23/6 (June 2023).

[27]L Beslie, 'El Salvador's Experiment with Bitcoin as Legal Tender' (July 2022) National Bureau Of Economic Research.

financed entirely by cryptocurrency[28] and has enacted a regulatory regime for all virtual asset transactions. Against this context, the article examines the approach to regulation of virtual asset transactions in the Cayman Islands.

C. Why is the Cayman Islands attractive for virtual asset service providers?

The Cayman Islands are founded on a political system that has enabled it to compete on the world financial stage.[29] The Islands have become the go-to destination for hedge funds, yacht and aircraft registrations, captive insurance, and international banking.[30] The Caymans are home to 99 banks,[31] 116,996 companies[32] and 12,935 mutual funds[33] many of which will be crypto-related. The Cayman Islands political stability, regulatory and tax advantages have enabled corruption and abuse to be better resisted than in many offshore jurisdictions and ensure that the islands risk profile remains advantageous for the establishment of new enterprises. Furthermore, Cayman is continually demonstrating to the international political and financial community that they are active participants in the fight against money laundering and economic crimes. Cayman is one of the few jurisdictions in the world to be fully compliant with all 40 of 'FATF's Recommendations' and have a robust beneficial ownership regime in place. Yet despite this the Cayman Islands remains on the FATF and European grey lists. This is a paradox in AML regulation. Reasons for inclusion could include Cayman's location between cocaine producers in South American and the markets into which it is sold; The exponential growth in Cayman's offering in financial services; The inherent prejudice of international financial and taxation regulators in relation to offshore jurisdictions based upon the perceived opportunities for money laundering through corporate structures and tax evasion;[34] An additional reason could also be the want of the international regulatory community to see prosecutions take place for the perceived level of money laundering within the jurisdiction.

However, it can be clearly demonstrated that the Cayman Islands have moved to an age of increased regulation and that as an offshore jurisdiction they are active participants in the prevention of international crime. Issues surrounding taxation also need to be put aside by regulators such as the Organisation for Economic Co-operation and Development (OECD) and the onshore world needs to act against perceived tax avoidance or to reform their systems in a way that allows a level playing field in respect of tax matters[35] and not conflate them into offshore regulatory issues. Finally, the Cayman Islands regime has only been fully embedded over the last five years, it will take time

---

[28]https://www.caymancompass.com/2022/09/13/first-real-estate-sale-using-crypto-in-cayman/.

[29]AJ Perkins, 'Offshore Jurisdictions, Sunny Places for Shady Business No More' [2022] World Financial Review (September–October) 4.

[30]T Freyer and AP Morriss, 'Creating Cayman as an Offshore Financial Centre: Structure & Strategy since 1960' (2013) 45 Arizona State Law Journal 1297.

[31]<https://www.cima.ky/banking-statistics> accessed 26 September 2022.

[32]<https://www.ciregistry.ky/companies-register/company-statistics/> accessed 26 September 2022.

[33]<https://www.cima.ky/investment-statistics> accessed 26 September 2022.

[34]D Gunter and IH Giddy, *The International Money Market* (Prentice-Hall, Englewood Cliffs 1978); IS McCarthy 'Hosting Offshore Banks: Benefits and Costs' (May 1979) IMF Working Paper No 32 and OECD, *Harmful Tax Competition: An Emerging Global Issue* (OECD Publishing 1998), https://doi.org/10.1787/9789264162945-en

[35]AJ Perkins, 'Does Holding Offshore Jurisdictions to Higher AML Standards Really Assist in Preventing Money Laundering?' (2022) 25(4) Journal of Money Laundering Control 742–56.

for investigations and prosecutions to come forward. Yet if the KYC and other due diligence procedures are in place it may be that there isn't the perceived level of laundering within the jurisdiction. In any event, Cayman must remain at the forefront of these international initiatives to protect the integrity of its market economy in highly specialised financial products.[36]

In relation to cryptocurrencies, Cayman has been proactive in seeking to attract investment, but also to regulate it. When considering where to incorporate a company for the purpose of conducting virtual asset transactions, offshore jurisdictions are an attractive option. Cryptocurrencies are treated in the majority of onshore jurisdictions as financial assets. As such the profits gained through trading them are subjected to varying rates of capital gains taxation.[37] By setting up offshore, an entity dealing in virtual assets will make significant tax savings in relation to their investments. Offshore jurisdictions possess a range of corporate structures such as exempted companies, partnerships, foundation companies and trusts which are not subjected to a taxation regime. An intrinsic feature of virtual asset trading is the ability to trade in complete privacy. Therefore, incorporated entities who trade in virtual assets may decide to incorporate offshore because when converting currency or filing tax returns, the anonymity of those investments can be lost in the onshore world. Furthermore, offshore companies who trade virtual assets using multiple entities incorporated in different offshore jurisdictions, can add layers of protection to a trading algorithm by keeping their investment activities firmly within the offshore sphere and avoiding onshore reporting requirements.

Company, trust, banking, insurance, and their related laws make the Cayman Islands an attractive destination for virtual asset businesses to call home. The Cayman Islands Government promotes a pro-regulatory environment enhanced by its policy of open dialogue with the private sector.[38] The Islands also enjoy sophisticated infrastructure and an abundance of professional service providers. This offers economic and political stability to virtual asset entities wishing to incorporate in the jurisdiction. Furthermore, the existence of the Special Economic Zone (SEZ) in the form of the Cayman Commodities and Derivatives Park is designed to create a central global commodities and derivatives market within Cayman. SEZ Companies are incorporated under the provisions of the Special Economic Zone Act (2017 Revision) providing enhanced advantages for virtual asset entities who choose to call the Cayman Islands their jurisdictional home. An entity can incorporate as an SEZ Company if its principal purpose is to carry on business outside of the Cayman Islands.[39] An entity will be guaranteed incorporation within ten days and a jurisdictional undertaking is given to protect that SEZ Companies intellectual property. Additionally, SEZ Companies also gain exemption from direct or indirect taxation[40] and other regulatory fees such as trade certificate fees, work permit fees, customs and import duties, stamp duty fees, together with registration, filing and maintenance fees under the Partnerships Act (2013 Revision) and the Companies Act (2023 Revision).[41] In order to establish a physical presence within the jurisdiction SEZ Companies are also

[36] D Nedelcu, 'Money Laundering By Means Of Offshore Companies', Titu Maiorescu University Annals, Law Series, Year XVIII.

[37] For example in the UK see Check if you need to pay tax when you sell cryptoassets – GOV.UK (www.gov.uk).

[38] B Harrington, 'Trusts and financialization' (2017) 15(1) Socio-Economic Review 31–63.

[39] Section 18(1) Special Economic Zones Act (2017 Revision).

[40] Section 1(e) Schedule 3 Special Economic Zones Act (2017 Revision).

[41] Section 2 Schedule 3 Special Economic Zones Act (2017 Revision).

granted exemptions from the Cayman Islands stringent work permit requirements. Automatic initial five-year work and residency visas are granted to the directors and employees of the company.[42] Significant additional fiscal benefits also exist for SEZ Companies which include there being no investment restrictions on SEZ Companies allowing the directors to take decisions to hold, transfer, securitise, finance, raise security or list the legal or beneficial title of any or all the SEZ Companies equity.[43]

The Cayman Islands Government has clearly appreciated the importance of attracting fin tech business to the jurisdiction. There is a realisation that virtual asset business is essential to ensure the continued growth of Cayman as a global financial destination. However, in adopting this approach the Cayman Islands Government and its financial regulators need to ensure that the legislative space in which fin tech actors operate is structured around the highest possible regulatory standards. With demonstratable commitments to probity and transparency appropriate for the concerns that can accompany the presence virtual assets use in an offshore jurisdiction.

This article will now turn to outline the international standards expected of VASPs before moving on to evaluate the legislative regime enacted by the Cayman Islands Government in order to show commitment to those standards and to test their effectiveness.

I. The relationship of FATF with virtual assets and virtual asset service providers

By design, virtual assets were intended to be an alternative to the traditional forms of fiat currency. Naturally, this led to difficulties in how states should define and regulate virtual assets such as bitcoin. The FATF charged with developing effective measures to tackle money laundering and terrorist financing, took a keen interest in evaluating the extent to which virtual currencies are open to exploitation and subsequently led the charge for their regulation.[44]

The FATF's regulatory intervention began in 2013 with the issuing of the New Payments Products and Services Guidance. Surprisingly, the FATF did not concern itself with issues in relation to virtual assets nor address cryptocurrencies, which were already gaining significant market transactions. Instead, the FATF issued guidance as to the use of internet payment systems, encouraging states to develop private sector institutions to assess the risks of New Payment Providers and Services.[45] This was a soft and traditional starting point for the FATF, with it making commitments to promote a fuller understanding of the systems involved in convertible virtual currency and structure further discussion on the implementation of the FATF's traditional risk-based AML/CTF (counter-terrorist financing) approach to the virtual currency arena.[46]

The FATF's next regulatory intervention came in the form of its publication 'Virtual Currencies Key Definitions and Potential AML/CTF Risks'.[47] In a detailed and nuanced report the FATF took the proactive step of defining a virtual currency as a representation of value

[42]Section 3(1) Schedule 3 Special Economic Zones Act (2017 Revision).
[43]Section 20 Special Economic Zones Act (2017 Revision).
[44]M Egan, 'A Bit(Coin)of a Problem for the EU AML Framework' in CKing, C Walker and J Gurulé (eds), *The Palgrave Handbook Of Criminal and Terrorism Financing Law* (Palgrave Macmillan 2018) 183–208.
[45]FATF, 'Guidance for a Risk-based Approach Prepaid Cards, Mobile Payments and Internet Based Payment Systems' (June 2013) at para. 37.
[46]ibid at para. 29.
[47]FATF, 'Virtual Currencies: Key Definitions and Potential AML/CTF Risks' (June 2014).

that can be digitally traded, function as a medium of exchange, a unit of account or a store of value that does not have legal tender status. Such currency can be traded on an open or closed basis, this was intended to cover the broadest spectrum of currency uses in both the natural and virtual worlds.[48] This detailed definition was clearly intended by the FATF to be a position from which national regulators could begin to combat AML/CTF risks. The FATF identified such risks based upon the fact that virtual asset transactions could be conducted on a cross border basis allowing for anonymity as transactions were not conducted face to face, together with the ability to hold funds away from law enforcement authorities.[49] It is no wonder based on these statements some jurisdictions have taken a view that they should be banned and excluded from financial regulation[50] and gave the FATF further justification to intervene further in the virtual asset space.

That further regulatory intervention came when FATF released its traditional risk-based approach applying to virtual currencies that were convertible for fiat currency.[51] The FATF's intention was to aid responsible regulatory frameworks to support global AML efforts[52] and to ensure effective supervision of virtual assets. In seeking to set standards the FATF deployed its long-standing pillars of co-ordination mechanisms and the application of a risk-based approach[53] to virtual currencies. The FATF mandated virtual assets be regulated based upon the same principles as traditional financial institutions, and apply equivalent licencing and registration regimes.[54] States would also be required to enact sanctions regimes containing dissuasive civil, criminal and administrative sanctions for using virtual assets for the purposes of money laundering.[55] Those interacting with virtual currencies need to implement measures to obtain, hold and securely transmit originator and beneficiary information and to undertake customer due diligence and ensure participation in adequate record keeping and reporting of suspicious transactions.[56] These measures clearly are intended to mirror the KYC process in financial institutions and other sectors and impose the same virtues applicable to fiat currencies upon virtual assets.

To further clarify its risk-based approach, and to keep pace with the pace of change in the virtual asset arena the FATF published in 2019 its evolved guidance for 'A Risk Based Approach: Virtual Assets and Virtual Asset Service Providers'.[57] The FATF's new position marked an evolution in its approach and would pose significant challenges for the virtual asset industry. Helpfully, the FATF provided further clarification to the regulatory community as to the types of assets that should fall within their definition of a virtual asset. States should class virtual assets as including currencies, securities and other financial assets that can be digitally traded or transferred and can be used for payment

[48]ibid 4.
[49]ibid 9 and 10.
[50]Chambers-Jones (n 24).
[51]FATF, 'Guidance for a Risk-Based Approach to Virtual Currencies' (June 2015).
[52]B Scott, 'How Can Cryptocurrency and Blockchain Technology Play a Role in Building Social and Solidarity Finance?' UNRISD Working Paper No. 2016-1.
[53]E Helleiner 'The Politics of Global Financial Regulation: Lessons from the Fight Against Money Laundering' in J Eatwell and L Taylor (eds), *International capital markets: Systems in transition* (OUP 2002) 177–204.
[54]ibid paras. 23–32.
[55]ibid para. 38.
[56]ibid paras 35 and 36.
[57]FATF, 'Guidance for a Risk-based Approach Virtual Assets and Virtual Asset Service Providers' (June 2019).

or investment purposes.[58] This marks a clear distinction by the FATF from its 2015 approach and includes virtual asset to virtual asset transactions and virtual asset to fiat currency transactions and represents a broadening approach to virtual asset regulation.

Not only wishing to regulate virtual assets the FATF took the opportunity to expand the regulatory talons to those that provide services in relation to them. The FATF subjected VASPs to stringent regulation if they conducted any business that involved the exchange between virtual assets and fiat currencies, exchange between one or more forms of virtual assets, transfer of virtual assets, safekeeping and administration of virtual assets or instruments, participation in the provision of financial services related to virtual assets, and the sale of such assets.[59] Again this broad definition is intended to capture a range of entities that deal in virtual assets. The regulatory structure envisaged by the FATF for VASPs includes registration and licensing with a regulatory body.[60] Given the FATF's concerns about the virtual asset space, it is unsurprising that they have chosen a regulatory body to supervise the industry rather than suggest self-regulation. The VASP supervisory body is also to ensure that a sanctions regime is in place for failure to abide by the FATF's stringent AML and KYC policies,[61] with a requirement for VASP to submit suspicious activity reports where the requisite suspicion of money laundering is raised.[62] Sanctions are also expected where money laundering is detected, including funds and property being frozen or confiscated.[63]

By far the most controversial proposal contained in the FATF's 2019 recommendations in relation to the implementation of the travel rule. This rule requires VASPs to gather simultaneously and securely, details of the originator and beneficiary information in a virtual asset transaction. Such information should contain names, wallet addresses, account numbers, physical addresses, national ID numbers, IP addresses and transaction hashes.[64] The transposition of the travel rule into the virtual asset sphere caused significant concern because at the time of the FATF's proposal there were no mechanisms in place for this information to be exchanged between VASPs.[65] This poses a challenge for the industry because cryptocurrency transfers occur within blockchain, and the details required by the travel rule cannot be sent as part of those messages. Furthermore, the requirements of the travel rule will affect the speed of transactions and add significantly to the costs associated with virtual asset transactions in order to comply with additional AML and CTF requirements. Data protection issues are also prevalent with the proposals especially as the European General Data Protection Regulation (GDPR) does not allow the transfer of personal data to the United States.[66]

In 2021 because of material changes in the virtual asset arena and the emergence of decentralised finance the FATF issued 'Updated Guidance For A Risk Based Approach

[58]ibid para. 33(b).
[59]ibid para. 33(c).
[60]ibid paras. 67, 77–85.
[61]ibid paras. 90–107.
[62]ibid para. 109.
[63]ibid paras. 63, 70, 71 and 73.
[64]ibid 5.
[65]T Altankhuyag, 'The AML 'Travel Rule': A New Challenge for VASPs and GDPR' (2020)GRC World Forums <https://www.grcworldforums.com/financial-crime/the-aml-travel-rule-a-new-challenge-for-vasps-and-gdpr/236.article> accessed 10 September 2023.
[66]Transfer of data to the US requires additional guarantees according to Article 44 GDPR.

For Virtual Assets and Virtual Asset Service Providers'.[67] The FATF's focus on regulating virtual assets and their service providers within this guidance is based upon a functional approach rather than underlying technology, business category or custodial status. The meaning of a virtual asset is further enhanced and driven by technological advances to include central bank currencies, stable coins and non-fungible tokens. The FATF clearly wants the widest possible application of its AML principles to emerging technology and captures virtual assets that can be traded, transferred, used for payment or investment, or if the asset is a means of recording or representing ownership.[68]

The FATF maintains its functional approach when providing guidance as to the factors that would indicate that a business entity is a VASP. Factors for regulators include whether the entity operates in multiple jurisdictions, offers services in stable coin or higher risk virtual assets, and considers the application of AML CTF regimes and effective licencing.[69]

The FATF also provided further clarification as to the due diligence required by a VASP under the travel rule. The updated guidance covers transfers between VASPs and sets out the data that an originator and beneficiary must verify prior to completing a transaction for accuracy. This information includes names, account numbers and physical addresses of the originator and beneficiary.[70] Such records must also be retained for the purposes of sanctions screening. The goal is clearly to ensure that VASPs establish an audit trail for funds transfers and enable AML and other relevant controls be applied during the transfer process. The FATF also expanded the rules applicable to unhosted wallets and requires originator and beneficiary information on transactions from personal wallets.[71] Many have argued this step is unnecessary however, the FATF sees significant risk and therefore, has devised and mandated additional regulation. The FATF are clearly being robust in their expectations in relation to the travel rule and make clear that they expect jurisdictions to implement and enforce it in spite of the technological and procedural difficulties in implementation.

In 2023 the FATF produced its third review on the implementation of its standards in relation to virtual assets and VASPs.[72] The report makes for a sober assessment of international regulators attempts to comply with the FATF's standards with regulation of the virtual asset space lagging well behind other financial sectors.[73] Three quarters of jurisdictions surveyed are only partially or not compliant with the FATF's standards,[74] with up to one third of participants unsure on how to regulate the VASP sector. Travel rule implementation is weak with half of the jurisdictions surveyed having taken no steps to implement the rule.[75] The FATF are naturally concerned because this leaves virtual assets and their service providers vulnerable to misuse. However, these statistics should not be viewed as surprising. The FATF's guidance leaves states with a number of questions, firstly, where to locate supervisory

[67]FATF 'Updated Guidance for a Risk Based Approach for Virtual Assets and Virtual Asset Service Providers' (October 2021).
[68]ibid paras. 47–54.
[69]ibid paras. 55–94.
[70]ibid paras. 182 and 183.
[71]ibid para. 105.
[72]FATF 'Targeted Updated on Implementation of the FATF Standards on Virtual Assets and Virtual Asset Service Providers' (June 2023).
[73]ibid 2.
[74]ibid.
[75]ibid.

authority. Should this be with a single supervisor? A concurrent market regulator one focusing on AML and the other market integrity? Or in the alternative would it be best to set up a new supervisory body altogether? Secondly, the lack of implementation of the travel rule demonstrates the absence of technological solutions available and that the FATF have failed to appreciate the lack of centralisation in virtual asset models.[76] Whilst this may seem negative, all is not lost. The FATF's intervention in the virtual asset arena have given a much firmer basis for trust in the usage of these assets. There are good intentions to limit the risk of money laundering, to protect investors and consumers and to provide stability to an ever-growing virtual asset market.[77] However, the FATF whilst setting the bar high, may have set it too high in the absence of technological solutions, states should be given sufficient time to implement these standards and not face FATF sanction which any forward-thinking commercial jurisdiction is keen to avoid.

II. The Cayman Islands regulatory response to virtual assets and their service providers

The constant evolution of fin tech regulation has resulted in offshore financial regulators having to design and adapt regulatory frameworks to show compliance with international regulatory standards and to protect their valuable financial services industries. Examples abound, as will be outlined in the following paragraphs.

In Guernsey, the Financial Services Commission have taken a cautious approach by issuing stark warnings about the inherent risks associated with virtual assets. However, Guernsey have designed a legislative structure to allow virtual assets to become part of its financial offering. Guernsey subjects virtual assets and structures to the same regulatory criteria as tangible assets which ensures that there are key controls in place around custody, liquidity, valuation of assets, investor information together with compliance with AML/CTF laws.[78]

The Isle of Man Financial Services Authority has also had to grapple with the regulation of virtual assets as many providers and assets are incorporated in the jurisdiction. The Isle of Man offers virtual assets and their providers an abundance of secure data centres from which to operate together with an attractive tax and regulatory environment. It is therefore surprising that the Isle of Man has adopted a light touch approach to regulation. The Isle of Man's regulatory structure treats virtual assets as securities meaning that they will fall outside of regulatory oversight. However, virtual asset entities will need to ensure general compliance with AML/CTF requirements.[79]

Jersey has made significant amendments to its Proceeds of Crime Law in 2016 to include virtual currencies as a form of currency[80] and provide for virtual currency

[76] L De Koker, 'FATF's New Virtual Asset Service Provider Standards: An Important First Step' (2020) 27 Journal of Financial Crime 309.

[77] K Byttebier and K Adamos, 'Cryptoassets – a New Frontier for Money Laundering and Terrorist Financing: Legal Changes to Address the Increasing AML Risk' [2022] ahead-of-print Journal of Financial Crime. https://doi.org/10.1108/JFC-10-2022-0262.

[78] Guernsey Financial Services Commission <https://www.gfsc.gg/faqs-0> accessed 26 September 2022.

[79] Isle of Man Financial Services Authority, 'Guidance: Crypto Asset/ Token Activity Regulation' <https://www.iomfsa.im/media/2720/regulatory-perimeter-for-tokens.pdf>.

[80] Section 4(4) Proceeds Of Crime Law (Jersey).

exchange. Interestingly however, this legislative amendment does not include a definition of VASP.[81] Nonetheless, such entities are required to comply with the Islands law, regulation, and policies in relation to AML. This is an unusual development albeit not surprising given that the amendments to Jersey's laws were taken amidst a rising awareness to virtual assets and the potential risks that they pose.

The Cayman Islands have taken a sophisticated approach to the regulation of virtual assets and their service providers compared to other offshore jurisdictions. On one view it might be contended that this was done to achieve competitive advantage. However, it is more likely that Cayman is seeking to demonstrate to the FATF and OECD that it is moving to an increased level of regulation in relation to AML and CTF and is responding to international initiatives which ensure that major jurisdictions will not tolerate or do business with poorly regulated states. Furthermore, Cayman is seeking to demonstrate that, as an offshore jurisdiction, it is still an active participant in the prevention of international crime.[82] The Cayman Islands Government introduced a virtual asset framework in 2020. It is no coincidence that the enactment of the virtual asset regime followed Cayman's fourth round of mutual evaluation by the FATF.[83] Under the new framework any virtual asset structure that wishes to incorporate or trade in the Cayman Islands will have to comply with a plethora of legal requirements enacted in response to Cayman's AML reform agenda.[84]

The Virtual Asset (Service Providers) Act came into force in two distinct phases. Phase one focusing on AML/CTF issues came into force on 31 October 2020, with phase two focusing on licensing requirements entering into force in June 2021. The Cayman Islands has drafted its virtual asset and VASP framework to ensure that it is compliant with the AML recommendations of the FATF. This pathway was no doubt adopted by the government as a result of the Cayman Islands increased monitoring by the FATF. The legislative framework adopts the FATF's two-pronged approach of ensuring an adequate licensing regime and that appropriate money laundering controls are enacted.

Virtual assets are defined in the legislation as a digital representation of value that can be digitally traded or transferred and can be used for payment or investment purposes, but do not include a digital representations of fiat currencies.[85] This is a clear embedding of the correct focus upon transferability and exchangeability of such assets. This is intended to capture activities, rather than classes of virtual assets, and will apply to a broad range of assets including cryptocurrencies, security tokens, utility tokens and other virtual assets which are capable of transfer or exchange.

The provision of a virtual asset service is defined in the Act as involving an entity issuing and exchanging virtual assets together with any of the following activities which an entity could perform on or behalf of another party. These include exchange

[81]Section 9(2)(B) Proceeds Of Crime Law (Jersey).
[82]See n 30.
[83]CFATF, 'Anti-money laundering and counter-terrorist financing measures: Cayman Islands Mutual Evaluation Report' (2019).
[84]Legislation that a virtual currency business will need to comply with includes the Securities Investment Business Act (2020 Revision), The Mutual Funds Act (2021 Revision), The Private Fund Act (2021 Revision), The Money Services Act (2020 Revision), The Bank and Companies Trust Act (2021 Revision), The Proceeds of Crime Act (2020 Revision), The Proliferation (Prohibition) Financing Act (2017), Anti Money Laundering Regulations (2023 Revision), The Stock Exchange Companies Act (2014 Revision), and the International Tax Co-operation (Economic Subsistence) Act (2021 Revision).
[85]Section 2(1) Virtual Asset (Service Providers) Act (2022 Revision).

between virtual assets and fiat currencies or other virtual assets, transfers of virtual assets, custody services, participation in and provision of financial services related to a virtual asset issuance or the sale of virtual assets.[86] The focus of the legislation is upon a broad range of corporate entities which engage in virtual asset services for or on behalf of a third party. An entity will be deemed to provide virtual asset services, and require a licence if it engages in virtual asset trading, custody and issue of virtual assets and the provision of financial advice in relation to them. This does not prohibit natural persons from engaging in virtual asset transactions. However, there is a clear prohibition on carrying them out for another. The failure to register will also result in strict sanction which complies with the FATF's guidance to ensure that there are dissuasive sanctions in force to prevent money laundering.

Any entity[87] providing on a regular, occasional or on an intermittent basis virtual asset services must register with the Cayman Islands Monetary Authority (CIMA) before commencing operations. Virtual asset service activities include acting as a virtual asset custodian, an exchange business, carrying on activities that involve virtual asset tokens or investment funds that accept subscriptions in virtual assets or making redemptions.[88] A failure to register and carry on any of these activities will result in the imposition of a fine of KY$25,000 and potential imprisonment for up to one year on summary conviction. If trading continues following conviction, the fine increases by KY$10,000 per day for each day that the offence continues.[89]

A VASP will be treated as a relevant financial business[90] and subjected to AML regulation.[91] Thus it will be prohibited from becoming concerned in an arrangement where it knows or suspects the facilitation, acquisition, retention, use or control by on or behalf of another person of criminal property.[92] This statutory statement is a general prohibition upon a VASP becoming involved in money laundering activities. In addition, the prohibition is extended by virtual asset entities being prevented from aiding, abetting, counselling or procuring money laundering activities.[93] Therefore, in order to comply with its AML obligations, a VASP will need to implement KYC procedures as well as AML policies and procedures. As a matter of good practice, a VASP will be expected to appoint an AML compliance officer who will be responsible for ensuring the adoption of appropriate measures in order to comply with the AML regulations. They will also act as the point of contact for CIMA.[94] In addition, a VASP will be expected to also appoint an AML reporting officer.[95] This is so that internal procedures can be maintained for the reporting of suspicious activity and that there is a

---

[86]Section 2(1) Virtual Asset (Service Providers) Act (2022 Revision).

[87]Whether registered as a Company incorporated under the Companies Act (2023 Revision), a general partnership registered under the Partnership Act (2013 Revision), a limited partnership registered under the Partnership Act (2013 Revision), an exempted partnership registered under the Partnership Act (2013 Revision), a foreign company registered under Part IX Companies Act (2023 Revision), a limited liability company registered under the Limited Liability Companies Act (2012 Revision), a limited liability partnership registered under the Limited Liability Partnership Act (2021 Revision).

[88]Section 4 Virtual Asset (Service Providers) Act (2022 Revision).

[89]Section 35(1) and (2) Virtual Asset (Service Providers) Act (2002 Revision).

[90]Section 21 of Schedule 6 Proceeds Of Crime Act (2020 Revision).

[91]Confirmed in Section 9(3) (D) and (E) Virtua Asset (Service Providers) Act (2022 Revision).

[92]Section 134 Proceeds Of Crime Act (2020 Revision).

[93]Section 181 Proceeds Of Crime Act (2020 Revision).

[94]Section 3 Anti Money Laundering Regulations (2023 Revision).

[95]Section 33 Anti Money Laundering Regulations (2023 Revision).

designated officer who will report such activity to the Financial Reporting Authority.[96] VASPs will need to maintain a risk based approach so that financial activities are monitored and that appropriate policies and procedures are put in place in order to mitigate those risks.[97] Regulated entities will also need to maintain appropriate records of documentation and information not only to comply with the AML regulations but to also discharge obligations to maintain and comply with identification and verification procedures on an enhanced or standard basis.[98] It will also be essential to maintain adequate systems to identify risk in relation to persons, countries and activities. This should ideally include checks being made against applicable sanctions lists.[99] VASP businesses should also adopt appropriate risk management procedures concerning the conditions under which a customer may utilise the business relationship prior to verification.[100] There must also be stringent observation of countries, published by a competent authority, which are not compliant or do not sufficiently comply with the recommendations of the FATF.[101] VASP should also ensure that they implement internal controls to ensure that there are effective risk based communication functions, for the ongoing monitoring of the business relationship[102] and provide employee training on risks and procedures.[103]

Should any of these duties be breached directors, members, partners and managers of a VASP could find themselves liable for fines of KY$500,000 for breaches of the AML regulations (2023 Revision) and could even find themselves imprisoned for up to two years.[104] In addition to this harsh regime the CIMA can level administrative fines for non-compliance with the provisions of the AML regulations and the Virtual Asset Service Providers Act.[105] The draconian nature of the measures is no doubt intended to foster a culture of regulatory compliance and to demonstrate to the international community that breaches of the rules are taken seriously by the jurisdiction. The Cayman Islands regulatory framework treats VASPs as regulated financial business and subjects them to stringent AML regulation. The Cayman AML regulations require a VASP to comply with customer due diligence requirements. This will mean that VASPs will need to gather information in respect of the customer, the source of funds and beneficial ownership information. It may be possible that a VASP will be able to rely upon simplified due diligence procedures obtaining certified copies of passports, utility bills and corporate documentation. However, this can only take place where the payment is remitted from an account held by a customer in the Cayman Islands. A further difficulty is presented for a VASP in that, within Cayman, simplified due diligence cannot be applied for a one-off transaction. It is likely, therefore, each initial customer based upon the risk profile of virtual assets will need to be subjected to enhanced due diligence procedures. This will involve a VASP obtaining additional information from customers, verifying that information through

---

[96]Section 34 Anti Money Laundering Regulations (2023 Revision).
[97]Sections 8 and 9 Anti Money Laundering Regulations (2023 Revision).
[98]Part III Anti Money Laundering Regulations (2023 Revision).
[99]Section 5(v) Anti Money Laundering Regulations (2023 Revision).
[100]Section 16 Anti Money Laundering Regulations (2023 Revision).
[101]Section 5(vii) Anti Money Laundering Regulations (2023 Revision).
[102]Section 5(viia) Anti Money Laundering Regulations (2023 Revision).
[103]Section 5 Anti Money Laundering Regulations (2023 Revision).
[104]Part IV Proceeds Of Crime Act (2020 Revision).
[105]CIMA derives its powers from the Monetary Authority Act (2020 Revision), Monetary Authority (Administrative Fines) Regulations 2019, Proceeds Of Crime Act (2020 Revision) and the Anti Money Laundering Regulations (2023 Revision).

independent sources, keeping such information under constant review and monitoring on an ongoing basis.[106] Transactions entered into by an entity will also need to be screened to see if they meet the suspicion threshold and require reporting to the relevant authority.[107] Failure to comply with the prescriptive due diligence standards will result in harsh fines and potential imprisonment for the directors involved in an attributable act of neglect. CIMA also can levy substantial fines for non-compliance with the AML regulations or the Virtual Asset Service Providers Act. This should no doubt satisfy the FATF of Cayman's dissuasive sanctions regime and makes a clear commitment that money laundering will not be tolerated in the jurisdiction and will be punished harshly.

In full compliance with the FATF Recommendation 16, the Cayman Islands on 1 July 2022 enacted the travel rule. This requires that a VASP when transferring assets must collect and verify the name of the originator and beneficiary, together with account numbers or transaction numbers, government issued identification, date and place of birth in relation to each transaction.[108] This demonstrates more than lip service by Cayman financial regulators and shows that since Cayman's fourth round of mutual evaluation a culture of super compliance[109] is being embedded into the jurisdictions AML practices. As noted earlier Cayman has generally followed the FATF standards in reforming its regime. This means that when a VASP is transferring virtual assets to a beneficiary they are under an obligation to gather, verify and record information about virtual asset transaction. The travel rule was originally used by the Financial Crimes Enforcement Network in respect of fiat currency transfer. However, in May 2019, the FATF expanded the scope of this doctrine to cover VASP transfers of virtual currency.[110] The VASP industry is still grappling with how to comply with this drastic intervention by the FATF. The reason for this is that there is now a positive obligation on VASPs to collect information that is not necessary or contained within the blockchain transaction. An example would be the customer's name and address.[111] The Cayman Islands legislative regime requires a great deal more information requiring that the originator and beneficiaries account numbers, transactions numbers, address, government issued ID number and date and place of birth be provided simultaneously or concurrently with the transfer of any virtual asset.[112] This is an onerous obligation for any virtual asset transaction and the industry in the Cayman Islands has expressed concern that the rule may drive criminal users of such assets underground because they will move their transactions off controlled platforms.[113] However, these are just some of the wider structural issues that the FATF will need to deal with. Cayman at this stage is fully compliant with the travel rule provisions and need to ensure that they stay at the forefront of developments in respect of the rule in the coming years.

[106]Section 27 Anti Money Laundering Regulations (2023 Revision).
[107]Section F Guidance Notes (Amendments) on the Prevention and Detection of Money Laundering, Terrorist Financing and Proliferation Financing in the Cayman Islands (February 2021).
[108]Section 49(C) Anti Money Laundering Regulations (2023 Revision).
[109]A Travers, 'Super Compliance In The Cayman Islands' (2004) 19(5) J.I.B.L.R 186–88.
[110]FATF (n 57).
[111]K Kirkpatrick and others, 'FinCEN Travel Rule Updates Sets Challenge For Crypto' <www.law360.com/articles1207330> accessed 23 February 2023.
[112]Section K Guidance Notes (Amendments) on the Prevention and Detection of Money Laundering, Terrorist Financing and Proliferation Financing in the Cayman Islands (February 2021).
[113]M Gordan and others, 'Crypto Exchanges have 12 Months to Implement FATF Anti Money Laundering' <https://www.cliffordchance.com/insights/resources/blogs/regulatory-investigations-financial-crime-insights/2019/07/crypto-exchanges-have-12-months-to-implement-fatf-anti-money-laundering.html> accessed 23 February 2023.

There has also been an attempt by the Cayman Island legislature to future proof the VASP legislative regime, which is particularly important given that as blockchain technology continually adapts to market conditions. Under Part 3 of the Virtual Asset Service Providers Act[114] the CIMA is granted the power to grant a sandbox licence[115] for up to twelve months allowing innovative fin tech businesses to be licensed based on the principles of honesty, integrity and the fair treatment of customers[116] in the delivery of their services. This is to ensure that innovative fin tech can deliver services within Cayman and that, whilst doing so, those entities comply with global standards and best practices for combatting money laundering and terrorist financing. Importantly, CIMA is able to tailor the licence offered to a VASP under the sandbox regime and can limit the number of clients to whom services may be offered, impose reporting requirements, restrict the licensees advertising or include requirements for disclosures to be made to clients.[117] CIMA is able to revoke the sandbox licence where the activities of a VASP pose a material risk to the public and the stability of financial services within the Cayman Islands.[118]

Whilst there is much praise for the Cayman Islands VASP regime there are however, two areas of the legislative framework that could undermine the excellent work that Cayman is doing to prevent money laundering taking place via virtual assets within the jurisdiction. The first area of concern is the ease of access to registration as a VASP. The Cayman Islands possess stringent immigration and corporate registration standards. However, these have been significantly relaxed under the provisions of the Special Economic Zone Act (2017 Revision) granting significant advantages to a VASP who wishes to register in the jurisdiction. These include incorporation within ten days, which is quicker than I can open a bank account as an island resident, together with exemptions from work permit fees and customs and import duties. Offshore jurisdictions are frequently criticised by international financial regulators for their conscious efforts to attract business by allowing relatively free entry and by adopting a flexible attitude where taxes, levies and regulation is concerned.[119] Such criticism feels fully justified on this occasion. The Virtual Asset Service Providers Act provides robust regulatory standards for a VASP's interactions with virtual assets, however, the ease of access to the market undermines this regime. The Cayman Islands government should bolster its compliance standards by ensuring that a VASP is not given special treatment to incorporate in the jurisdiction and should subject them to the same level of scrutiny demanded by the VASP legislative regime.

The second area of concern relates to the regulatory sandbox licence that CIMA can grant for a period of up to one year allowing for innovative technology and its delivery channels to be developed. Caution should be taken with this sandbox regime. CIMA should only use it sparingly, and should ensure that the licence granted is stringently tailored, with significant monitoring covenants, and limits to the services that a sandbox entity can offer. Ambitions of the Cayman Islands becoming a fin tech financial hub and allowing developing financial technology easy access to the jurisdiction with a light touch regulatory approach should not happen until such a time as sufficient

---

[114]Sections 17–21 Virtual Asset (Service Providers) Act (2022 Revision).
[115]Section 18 Virtual Asset (Service Providers) Act (2022 Revision).
[116]Section 17 Virtual Asset (Service Providers) Act (2022 Revision).
[117]Section 20 Virtual Asset (Service Providers) Act (2022 Revision).
[118]Section 21 Virtual Asset (Service Providers) Act (2022 Revision).
[119]See fn 34.

regulation can be developed. Whilst the legal regime surrounding virtual assets is being pushed by the pace at which the technology is being developed, Cayman needs to remember that it will always be subjected to a degree of heightened scrutiny in respect of money laundering because of its position as an offshore financial centre. Cayman therefore, needs to ensure that it has strong money laundering controls in place which are capable of comprehensively assessing the risk posed by virtual assets and their service providers as technology continues to evolve the regulatory landscape. Rather than grant a hasty sandbox licence to deal with emerging technology, Cayman policy makers should take time to reflect and design and plan a system and evolve the legislative framework that effectively mitigates the risks of that technology.

D. Conclusion

As the world's fifth biggest banking centre and the second largest captive insurance market,[120] the Cayman Islands attracts regular scrutiny from international financial regulators. The intense level of scrutiny is no doubt caused by the Islands tax neutral status and the perceived lax regulatory environment. Indeed, following the FATF's fourth round of mutual evaluations, in February 2021 Cayman was added to the so-called grey list (or jurisdictions under increased monitoring).[121] Given the repercussions of such international action, it comes as no surprise that there has been swift enactment of a legislative regime to regulate inter alia, virtual assets and their service providers.

It is important then that the Cayman Islands is seen by the international regulatory community to take active steps to ensure that appropriate measures are in place and that has been apparent since grey listing in February 2021, with significant efforts domestically to reform and enhance the AML/CTF regime. Given the harsh criticism of cryptocurrencies and their use in money laundering activities, it may come as a surprise that pseudo anonymous trading is being welcomed into the jurisdiction. However, the crypto economy has provided individuals with an exploding form of financialisation creating opportunities for enterprise development to take place, in the hope of creating network effects and peer to peer economic mobilisation in the crypto economy.[122] This creates a revenue stream from which offshore financial centres, such as Cayman, can profit by providing legal, accounting and corporate services leading to the establishment of a burgeoning economy. In turn, this can result in the creation of an obligation on financial regulators to, first, to design a legislative plan that effectively mitigates the risks created by dealing in virtual assets. Second, put in place strong money laundering controls that encourage VASPs to undertake comprehensive risk assessments as to their dealings with virtual assets.

Thus, while Cayman has reformed its AML regime, it remains to be seen how the international community, specifically the FATF, views Cayman's approach towards virtual assets. The initial steps taken by the FATF in its role as standards setter has encouraged jurisdictions to adopt specific standards in relation to virtual assets and VASP regulation.

[120] J Fichtner, 'The Cayman Conundrum: Why is One Tiny Archipelago the Largest Financial Centre in Latin America and the Caribbean?' <https://blogs.lse.ac.uk/usappblog/2017/11/11/the-cayman-conundrum-why-is-one-tiny-archipelago-the-largest-financial-centre-in-latin-america-and-the-caribbean/> accessed 13 September 2023.

[121] At the time of writing, Cayman is still on the list, but is expected to be removed at the October 2023 FATF Plenary.

[122] IH-Y Chiu, 'Regulating Crypto-Finance: A Policy Blueprint' ECGI Report' <https://ecgi.global/content/working-papers>.

Indeed, the FATF's efforts through various virtual asset focused guidance should be viewed as a positive step in the development of a first step approach to globally regulating virtual assets and their service providers. However, the FATF's evolving guidance still leave jurisdictions complex regulatory questions to answer at a national level. These include issues such as where is best to locate supervisory authority for virtual assets and VASPs, and how to create sufficient regulatory capacity within financial supervisory systems that enable regulators to identify, assess and monitor the risks associated with virtual asset transactions.

Virtual asset technology is a rapidly evolving field that has secured significant investment and global traction. Determining an appropriate regulatory structure to balance the economic potential of virtual assets whilst mitigating against the anonymity risks that they pose is a challenge that financial regulators are having to quickly grapple with. When these virtual assets are then combined with transactions in offshore jurisdictions international regulators will no doubt have a degree of scepticism about the regulatory structures surrounding those interactions because offshore jurisdictions are essentially held to higher standards because of their offshore status.

Offshore jurisdictions need to have a robust approach to the regulation of virtual assets and not to be seen to encourage a race to the bottom in terms of regulation. Regulatory structures need to be designed so that when there are virtual asset transactions taking place offshore there is a system in place that gathers the full spectrum of information needed to identify the transferer and beneficiary together with the source of those funds. This is the only way to make certain that virtual currencies become an unattractive system for money launderers. If offshore jurisdictions can ensure that there are stringent standards for the virtual asset industry it may legitimise the uses of virtual assets and spur addition of these technologies within the traditional financial sector.[123]

Offshore jurisdictions need to evolve their financial offerings as technology changes but in doing so they need to strike a careful balance between having effective regulatory standards in place, against allowing easy access to the jurisdiction through the advantages that offshore incorporation can bring. Given the scepticism with which offshore jurisdictions are viewed by international financial regulators, places like the Cayman Islands should not be seen to sell the shovels with which to further expand the fin tech industry. Particularly if those practices will lead to harmful money laundering practices being given an environment in which to promulgate.

Acknowledgement

Andrew wishes to thank Professors Amy Wallace and Colin King and Tommy Hoogaars for their kind comments on this work. Any errors are naturally my own.

Disclosure statement

No potential conflict of interest was reported by the author.

[123]GC Velkes, 'International Anti Money Laundering Regulation of Virtual Currencies and Assets' (2020) 52 New York University Journal of International Law and Politics 875.

Index

Note: Endnotes are indicated by the page number followed by 'n' and the endnote number e.g., 20n1 refers to endnote 1 on page 20.